COLLECTED POEMS

P.J.KAVANAGH
Collected
Poems

CARCANET

First published in 1992 by
Carcanet Press Limited
208-212 Corn Exchange Buildings
Manchester M4 3BQ

A CIP catalogue record for this book
is available from the British Library
ISBN 0 85635 973 4

The publisher acknowledges financial assistance
from the Arts Council of Great Britain

Typeset in 10pt Palatino by Bryan Williamson, Darwen
Printed and bound in England by SRP Ltd, Exeter

Contents

ONE AND ONE (1959)

12   Dedication Poem
13   Love Poem
13   'Little Men, at Work'
14   St Thomas More
16   *'Arbeit Macht Frei'*
17   To Darkness and to Me
17   Narrative
19   Natural History
20   Serenade for Sally
20   Declaration of Dependence
21   Christmas Holiday
21   Sad Song
22   Recollected in Tranquillity
23   This Pilgrim by the Rhône at Avignon
24   Yeats's Tower
25   Handsome is as Handsome Does
26   Speech from an Unwritten Play
26   Beggar at the Villa d'Este
27   Intimations of Unreality
28   Lamentation of a Broken Silhouette
29   'Nothing is Easy'
30   Merton Garden
31   Memo to Travellers
32   Sonnet
33   Niobe
33   Gardens are Lonely Places
34   A Refusal to Mourn Fashionably
34   The Deep-sea Trends
35   The Perky Traveller Ponders
36   'While Three Men Stand Together'
37   At a Public Rejoicing
37   The Words of Mercury to a Muse
38   The Devil Speaking
39   Visitation

ON THE WAY TO THE DEPOT (1967)

43   Saint Tropez
43   *Dominus Illuminatio Mea*
44   Lines for my Father

45   Plain Tale from the Hills
46   The Spring
47   August by the River
47   Watch this Space
48   Wherever You Are
49   Westwell Churchyard, Oxfordshire
50   Sequence
53   On the Way to the Depot
54   Afternoon in Sneem
56   The Temperance Billiards Room
56   In the Rubber Dinghy
57   Perfection Isn't Like a Perfect Story
58   Not Being a Man of Action
59   Satire I (after Sir Thomas Wyatt)
62   *Diptyque touristique*
63   Goldie *sapiens*
63   May
64   No One
65   Deathday
66   Closing Down
68   *Conversations with Eckermann*
69   Birthday
70   Surviving
71   And Odysseus Wept
72   Moving

ABOUT TIME (1970)
75   One
79   Two
81   Three
83   Four
86   Five
89   Six
91   Seven
97   Eight
99   Nine
101   Ten

EDWARD THOMAS IN HEAVEN (1974)
109   Occasional Birds
110   Sometimes
110   For Bruno

111   October
112   Commuter
113   The Day of the Shoot
114   Eclogue
118   Game
118   The Famous Poet
119   Sentimental Education
120   Lover of Quietness
121   Consolations
122   Real Sky
124   Winterpraise
125   November the First
125   A Box of Sons
126   Like the Heron
127   All I Want
128   Child's Walk
128   Spencer Park
129   Driving Back
129   Opened and Fastened
130   Picture a Father
131   And Light Fading
131   Edward Thomas in Heaven
132   The Clapham Elephants
133   Sporting Occasion, Korea
134   A Walk, a Small Event, a Dream
136   Just Now

LIFE BEFORE DEATH (1979)
139   Dome
139   For Bruno
141   Winter Hillside
141   Father and Son
142   Snapshots of New York and Hillsdale, N.Y.
143   While the Sun Shines
144   The Odd-job Hunter
144   Where You Watching Are
145   A Single Tree
146   Don't Forget the Keeper, Sir
146   A Great Gale, 1976
148   Breakfast in Italy
149   Ivor Gurney
151   Spoleto 1967

152 'A few still believe in heavenly reunions'
153 News from Gloucestershire
154 The Dead
154 Simile
155 After Reading the Life of Arthur McMurrough Kavanagh 1831-1889
157 Vespers, and Notices, at Prinknash Abbey
158 Gardening
158 Beyond Decoration
159 The Moon in Charge
160 Sun Overcast
160 Elder
161 Dandelion
161 Memory
163 On Giglio
164 Pilgrims
164 Borris House, Co. Carlow
165 For C.E.K.
166 Spring Arrival
167 Bread-and-Butter Letter
167 Praying
168 Seal
168 Illness
169 Air

PRESENCES: NEW POEMS (1987)
173 A Small World
174 Late Acknowledgement
175 Farmworker
175 *Ars est celare artem*
176 Birth of Middle Age
177 Walmer Castle
178 Politics
178 Birthday Visit
179 A Father Reorganises
180 Prayer in Middle Age
180 Heysel Stadium
182 Token
182 Drifts
185 Beside the Bed
186 Snowdrops
186 Nature Poet
189 Constitutional

AN ENCHANTMENT (1991)

193   A Ghost Replies
193   The Burning Bush
194   Levels
194   For Saint Cecilia
195   The Old Notebook
197   Autumn
198   Memorial Service
199   Chaos at Air Control
200   No More Songs
200   January Evening
201   Blackbird in Fulham
201   They Lift their Heads
202   Minimal Prayer Suggestion
203   In 'The Anglesea' Afterwards
205   Natural History
205   Invitation
206   Afflatus
207   Hope
208   Cardinal Bird, West Virginia
209   Calm in New York
209   Falklands, 1982
210   Whitsun
211   Resistance
211   Timesong
212   ITMA
213   In the Middle of the Wood
213   The Belt
214   Written in the Margin
216   Severn *aisling*
220   Message

221   Index of First Lines

ONE AND ONE

(1959)

Dedication Poem

Curled in your night-dress on the beach,
Corn-yellow ghost, pale with sleep,
Head to the starry North, bare toes to the burning East,
Tracking the sun's climb into our seaside perch,
I watch you at the fringe of this other island
Our public love makes private for us two;
Your face in floating shadow like a moon,
Stretching your arms around the bay to yawn,
Ebony trees in your fingers turning to green.
I stand alone, in the dark, with the birds in the bush.
Like the pewter lagoon I am flustered by day,
Which turns, turns, like a pin to prick out my eye.
Now Sun, the angry bo'sun, straddles the sea.
'Is that you?' your murmur,
Grateful and blind my whisper,
'You and me'.

Bali-Djakarta 1958

Love Poem

Can you forgive the fastidious cannibal
His unusual pleasures? Does your charity
Embrace the noisy whore, forgetting her manners
In front of your daughter? The cocky-walker
Who teaches your wife to care about clothes again
And look in the mirror? And yet defend
Your wife from your enemy and your daughter
From the convincing whore, your life from the cannibal?
When you can do this, and this, and lose
Your wife, your life and always your curious daughter,
Then we may talk of love and what we mean.

'Little Men, at Work'

Little men, at work, reconcile me to the great.
                                                    – Alfieri

Dogs barking. Men with guns.
The foul canal, brown-swollen by the rains,
Is lined with trigger-happy mothers' sons.
And not one simple man to clear the stinking drains.

Above my window cockney-sparrows build...
Hard to doubt the gay congruities,
Hard to live without complacencies.
Things are just as bad as we were told.
These busy squatters seem accomplices –
Straw from a beak blurs the page as I write.
Out in the street this morning there was a fight.
One of the men fell jerking in a fit.
I took my watching white-face on my well-shod feet
Down to my garden gate.
One barefoot watcher looked at me and spat.
Well, build from spittle and sparrow-straw bricks for a song!
Why, when it is impossible to Belong
Do all of us long for that more than anything?

13

Perhaps to write and rhyme a sense of loss
Makes one isolation briefly less.
Steel-helmets make that seem ridiculous.

For us no quasi-romantic State of War:
You scarcely notice when you live with fear.
If little lights were little one by one
Could any of Europe's bonfires have lasted for long...?
But who has words to say all that again?

Meanwhile the dogs are barking. Sentries yawn.
Someone, somewhere, switches the street-lights on.
Domestic sparrows end where they began.
We must leave tomorrow to the morning.
Perhaps tomorrow we shall wake up grown.
For if some bayonet or bomb cuts short the growing,
We know that nobody's better off, and that's worth knowing.

Djakarta, 1958

St Thomas More

In *Utopia* Thomas More
Suggested blandly that before
They should be allowed to marry,
Lest imaginings miscarry,
Truth would call it only fair
Couples saw each other bare.
Wise Thomas did not only mean
Naked bodies should be seen.
Bodies coupled are *pro tem*
As lonely dreams prefigure them.
No more, no less. The rough delight
Of talking in the flesh is right
And proper, if we but confess
Our undiminished loneliness.
It's good enough if we don't strain

14

To make a little love explain
All the nursery doubts that creep
Up our fingers while we sleep.
Because if our demand's too tall
Love wanly proves again that all
Love and arithmetic can do
Is prove that one and one make two.
Well Thomas knew this and he meant
Something more intelligent.
'Off, off you lendings' love in Lear
Cried aloud and that is near
The Thomas meaning; we may guess
A more than physical undress.
So lovers that are truly nude
Wear neither clothes nor attitude.
Identify the bogus swain:
It is he who will complain
That his object is unkind.
Does he mean he cannot find
One whose self-concern is such
It won't disturb his own too much?
Or, if requited, love's his glass
Where he and selfhood gaily pass
A gracious forenoon. Thus they play
At mental self-abuse all day.
And do not think this ruse antique.
Love dies in that way every week.
That love is blind the ancients knew
And Thomas only tried to show
What Socrates had known before,
That Love's a ladder not a law,
And our active verb 'to live'
Cannot stay intransitive.
But up the ladder see him climb
Who learns by heart Love's paradigm.
'I am I until I die
And must not make another take
My own image for my sake.
You are you and what we do
Together will not ever seem
Empty, a narcissus dream
If we but remember this

And mark division with a kiss.'
Good St Thomas, lest I stray
Further from the simple way
That you, less prolix, would suggest
By a daughter shown undressed,
I must end.
Be kind and send
Your blessing upon one who tries to show,
At length, the truth of what he does not know.

'Arbeit Macht Frei'

Inscription above the gate
of Auschwitz concentration camp
For Czeslaw Milosz

Young people dazed with love in dying countries
are unable to make connection between their beauties
and the truth of the smelling smoke they asked about
that stains your clothes and hair and never comes out
however you wash or kiss; the man with foreign features
who answered them and ravaged their belief
in whatever it was they trusted, in their own natures,
yawned at their anger and horror, found them naïf.
How older he seemed than the elders of their homeland!
They wanted to ask him a regimen to prevent
their sweet desire cloying their palates to rage
and driving their logic to bonfires when it was spent.
But he left them in silence, to decorate the cage
they no longer called a bower, but understood
was built of greed and was their chance of good.
They learned the cruelty in passion, in a lover,
was chaining them not only to each other.

To Darkness and to Me

For Br Humbert O'Donovan, O.P.

All day a tidy wind has filled the air
With last reluctant leaves like brittle birds.
But now like rats they settle and shift in corners.
Even the playing shadows seem to lack
Innocence, coupling on the winter stones.

Tree-blown the tethered shapes snap, and return,
Their clandestine elopements always doomed,
Each horizontal journey circumscribed
By rules of place and growing. And the stain
Spills on the pavement darkest at the root.

Seeming a shadow in a world of winds,
Hostile to me and each other, cold as money,
No liberating gust, I know, will shake
Me like an angel from the tread-mill
Prayer-wheel circle of my make.

O warming darkness growing deep to love!
Your somewhere-secret roots would have us grow
Fragrant and unquestioning as pines.
But I, Didimus, mistrust, and must explore
The wound around my birth; while every day
Your shadow lengthens on my puzzled earth.

Narrative

I dreamt a love-story yesterday.
Who loved who is anyone's guess.
But it tasted of love, and I still see
The little boy in the Scripture class.

'Thou shalt not...' 'Teacher, I don't want to.'
'How can you tell, vainglorious boy!
All men do.' 'Then I shall too.
If I can't tell, how can I say?'

Uncensored sunlight taught him extravagance,
Dancing in chalk-dust. His heart was the drum.
Warnings were winter. Dangerous innocence
Ticked its message, 'I'm a bomb.'

Much later, in a public place,
He kissed his fellow in the face.
A broken jaw, a troubled dream,
Wonders that will never cease.

He felt he was enclosed in glass
As streams divided round his head
Of pavement men as blind as grass.
He asked a tart if he was mad.

He lent his coat. The day grew cold.
A man had four. He borrowed one.
Forgot to ask him if he could.
Men heard of this, put out his sun.

Alone, alone in his premature coffin
He foundered low and pondered long.
Badgered the priest to visit him often,
Draw him a diagram where he went wrong.

'Patience! Patience!' sang the priest.
Begged him bow and pray for grace.
Promised him the Eucharist.
So he bowed and prayed at last.

He enjoyed resignation, it lightened his head,
Filled his eyes, like moons, with light.
He felt better. Said he did,
And opened his mouth to take the bread.

How could I know why he did it?
Perhaps to be hated was better than nothing.
The priest brought his hand to his mouth, and he bit it.
That noise of bone on bone. It broke my dreaming.

Did stars of comfort rain from the blows on his head?
That he blessed the warders, I'm sure, through teeth bright red.
Night picked him like a flower. I left him dead,
Still biting the hand that fed, that fed.

Natural History

Lambs bleat a lexicon of need
Whose adulthood is munch and fluke and death.
Preoccupied by wind their mothers feed
The cruelly butting heads and keep their breath
For belching and rebuke. They know the end:
He to be proud of his terminal difference,
She of her power to love her own. They tend
To agree about this for lack of evidence.
With the bleak complicity of years
They plot to taint their offspring as they run,
And brake them in to walking-pace careers
To reassure the selves a maggotting sun
Infected with doubt and bot. They cast their guilt
When children live in lies their parents built.

Serenade for Sally

the lights beneath her skin are gold
like buttercups beneath the chin
madonna lilies gleam above
tender lines of bone are hung
with summer flags with irises
violets of christmas turn
in the moulding of her eye
she is death's antithesis
time itself shall cherish her
knowing better than to try
the granite bloom of innocence

Declaration of Dependence

My love is like a river as she flows;
I trim it featly bobbing in the flood.
Where we shall arrive at neither knows,
Certain shipwreck every lap confides.
Questions on the way or run aground
Are out of order like my steering gear.
In the Aeolian cordage of my mind
Gusts of self-approval make the sound
Of sirens singing in a hero's ear.
No use to tell this drunken helmsman now
Spurning the omens, scum upon the wrack,
That while before his preening prow
Her waters part,
They meet behind his back.
You're not the only wise, whose sails are slack.

Christmas Holiday

In the december graveyard blossom moved
against remembering stone, softer than snow.
Along the christmas river we surprised
buds in the act of daring, sweet as toffee;
fields lay stretched and steaming in the sun,
and smoke was neat as feathers on the sky.
But discandying breath was only held. We felt
the afternoon turn over in its sleep
restless before it woke and blew us elsewhere
to practise separation like a scale
over and over until we run foolish,
to hoard and stroke the past till Now is gone,
to forget the past is now or not at all.

Sad Song

June her danäe shower lets fall
Over the purple judas tree.
On me her coins are wasted, all
Flowers are premature for me.

Wiser to take them, spend them, go
Richer to winter as men count?
Perhaps I would if I could but so
Make winter longer by that amount.

For my true summer is away.
No sun can understudy her.
With all my sweet in one bouquet
I must defy glib Lucifer.

She has her seasons, solstices,
Rich and sour, bright and black.
But though my system's Ptolemy's
I use her heart for almanac.

And so my truth keeps bright, the shine
Dulled only by the fear that she
Spends two summers, hers and mine,
Kissing beneath a judas tree.

Recollected in Tranquillity

I picked a cabbage rose
Of Renoir colour
For my girl.
She brushed her cheek with it.
We walked. The rose
Enfolding us,
Quite futureless, together.
Later
In the well-known room
We filled
Its leaves with yellow wine
And drank,
And kissed.
Cool as a cave
The rose against our cheeks.
I see her still
On occasions.
We continue to talk
Of some things.
We behave
Politely towards each other.

This Pilgrim by the Rhône at Avignon

When day begins too lucid and his sun
Sharpens outlines like a honing stone
This pilgrim seeks for rest among the shade
Of provençal renaissance arbours. But as he expected
Fails to find it. Which is no one's fault but his alone.
Non-pilgrims, who demand much from him, might be shocked
To learn he longs for rest as much as they do,
And would be all three monkeys when he hears
The most he can be sure of recited by the river:
No going back, but on, to disappearance...

Perhaps to ask too many questions
Is almost as great a mistake as to ask too few,
Since asking at all begs a dishonest answer.
But not to ask, or escape the asking, is worst.
What seems reality, gulped in crude doses,
Can postpone question-time. Tufts of hair
In a girl's armpit can fill with a kind of hubris
The frightened romantic fallen in love with acceptance.
Maybe such violence is out of fashion.
There are other ways. But he who elects to live
In the beckon of an intermittent sun has no escape.
Even his envy of this guiltless, named and destined water,
Turns to sulky recognition of another unsought warning
Whispered from the glacier through two countries,
Until like sweat through pores at last it passes
Into warm earth's cold shroud of sea, its enemy...

On its way it salutes the walls of this ancient city,
Where, for too long, a church which claims to be One,
Universal and Apostolic was none of those things
For too long.
                    The pilgrim's bewildered purpose
Is a healthy flood that washes obscuring dust
From possibly gnomic stones. But reveals
Only the seedless walls of the public ways
Prepared by the past; which nobly assist his walking
But muddle his destinations till he longs
To be Adam again, sometimes collects Kaffir masks,

Or goes to the U.S.A., studies the papers for his birthday sign,
And or raises a family just the size of himself,
Who come to use daddy's scrip for games in the attic.

But still he sniffs the truth like meals to come.
And if he talks of God we hear him cry,
'His presence escapes me like sweat!'
But these are the glands permit him live or else
He must splash in a tub or return, a detestable landfish,
To the cold stomach of the lightless sea, his enemy.

Yeats's Tower

The rain is the same.
Some of the trees original.
Certainly the stream
Is the one that woke you, lulled you,
The tiny bridge identical.
And what has happened since you climbed the stair
Would neither have surprised nor killed you.
Behind that outhouse wall you kept your car,
Deprecatingly – salaried senator,
Which took you south in the winter
To die, advisedly, before the war.
I was a child when you died
And now I stand beside
What remains of the tower
You took your gift inside
To raise it like a chalice,
Maliciously smiling, out of reach of malice,
Over the small and sour
Country of your birth;
Over the lunatic earth.
The roof and the floors are gone.
Stolen your sea-green slates,
And smithy-work from Gort.
Your blue distempers run
In cobalt-coloured rain.

You will forgive the thought
That made me in your hall
Write with a tinker's coal
My small and grateful name.
Things being as they are
You'll understand the fear
That I may never pass this way again.

Thoor Ballylee, August 1957

Handsome is as Handsome Does

With a sore on the tip of my nose
I stare up at a jagged streak of blue,
Untidy parting in the head of houses
Which is the world I change my shirt and sing for.
Don't misunderstand. I don't feel sorry for me,
Especially, but for us.
We've all got lungs that long to shout down silence
Were we ever allowed to hear it,
Limbs to stir the air into rhyme and reason
Matching and chasing our gestures, cut to our figures,
If it ever stayed still for us long enough to try.

No silence to carve our names on. No gloving air.

Take life as you find it, the murderer said.

Speech from an Unwritten Play

What do you see on the underside of leaves?
A fairer colour? Or a simile
for hair blown back by a similar wind?
Tell me. Take my hand.
There. And tell me. I should like to know
exactly. So hard to be precise.
I spend my life sitting at this window,
I am much alone, and as I watch
I wonder what my friend would make of it,
what you would say at the end
of our watching together, when we turned
having seen each other at last in all that beauty,
that frightening waste. You think it a waste
it is oh yes a waste and I am wasted
watching leaves that die and reappear
again and again the same above and below
but I am not the same no never
not for two minutes the same I do not know
who I am but who we are I know
when we are together. No.
Do not remove your hand. I do not permit it.

Beggar at the Villa d'Este

No legs. I must sit still.
People pass who are,
More or less, amused at falling water,
Treasures of this hill.
He was rich. I'm poor,
But share his pleasures.
I shan't risk my virtue for Perhaps,
When here expensive fancies are secure.
'It's obsessive – the fountains – the whole idea'
That posh-faced tourist says.
I have to laugh

At fear afraid of fear.
'Then you love water you mean?
The more fool you,' I say.
(He's much too tall to hear).
I was born near Lake Trasimene.
Nearly every evening that expanse
Of land-turned-liquid
Turns to grey to green,
Flamingo to bloody carmine.
There's no sense
In frightening one like that!
In all those colours, reeds like dead men's fingers
Break silences and mirrors.
I tell you there's no laughing on those banks,
On any beach or shore or not for long.
You get to think. Say prayers even.
Ugh! It cares a lot for you! No thanks!
But here's a prince, a cardinal, fly as they come,
By tricks and cheats puts water in his purse,
Makes something you can drown in, something cruel,
Dance in front of him like a hired fool.
Then you forget you have no legs. That's art.
Made him, they say, forget he had no heart.

And yet his house is damp. . . . And yet it's grand! . . .
If I could walk I'd go
As far from water as there is and oh!
If I could fly, as far away from land!

Intimations of Unreality

A square-skulled moonfaced monotone fowl,
because it is twilight has caught my eye
and slowly insultingly turned its neckless back.
Snubbed by an owl.
One skirt hem of the sky is torn by day still.
Night continues to mend it, ignoring me.
As I move, nervous against my reason,

27

there are rustles and splashes I cannot mistake for goodwill.
Blind white moths half my finger-nail size
zig-zag about my feet about no business.
I catch one in my hand, just to make contact
with some part of a world that's mine as well.
It even disdains to flutter,
but waits till I open my hand, then goes on as before.
I feel as though I, hungry,
have entered a room
where there was only just enough to go round.
Because I live in brick and change my clothes
must I allow the world and sky to ignore me?
Stay, Light! There is something you showed then that I missed!
Well then come, Dark! In your tunnel I'll be more watchful.
What did the river say?
     Ordeal by bats is beginning.
How cold this dew is!
     So it is really true then
That I neither inhabit this world, nor any other?

Lamentation of a Broken Silhouette

The nape of my neck is crusted with sugar like clinker;
But no one tastes or even sees it which
Is because from in front it's invisible,
From side and back it has a changing shape.
This chill-wind world cuts my shape into lines
So quite devoid of meaning, so shortest-distance
Between two vanishing points I do not wonder
No one takes my sugar when I bow.
Warm in the crook of an embracing elbow
My neck is round at last but alas
The rest of me falls away and I can't find it.
At any given moment what I can gather
Together I give to you. I quite understand
The malentendu and malice my pieces provoke.
I will even try to accept what love is going
For bits I bring that do not belong to me.

'Nothing is Easy'

Nothing is easy. Pity then
The poet more than other men.
— James Stephens

A vision invented me and she said this:

Come and live in my cave and be cold as a northern pool,
be hungry, but not any hungrier
than you are,
and much more proud.
We shall play all day at public ritual games
you'll find you're rather good at,
though no one standing by will tell you so.
No one else is there.
You see, most lovers beat at me with balloons
loaded with adjectives meant to stagger me.
Or they cut me into crystals with reflection
of things not allowed in my cave.
Not much is.
Round the mouth of it they complain,
fighting to keep themselves warm,
and to show me their valour and hatred of my detractors.
How funny! They don't even know what I really look like,
yet they will follow me always, so they swear,
(as if I went anywhere!)
but not, of course, inside my cave
where no mirrors are!

I wanted to ask just one question,
(it seemed a lonely life).
She forgot me and I disappeared.

Merton Garden

These walls infect the air
With pale nostalgia.
See, through the garden comes
That languished Lady under whose black thumbs
Our past grows waxen fruit
Our present cannot eat,
And fades, and dies.
Listen, (and argue). She never says but sighs:
'Stone upon stone well and truly laid
In noble manner now forgotten –'
(The stones themselves are rotten.) –
'Tops of the trees ruffle like sleeping birds
A bitter generation has no words
To consecrate the meaning of this garden.'

Well then, let us on this meaningful,
Ancient, uncomfortable,
Breeze-petalled seat,
Catalogue some things She misses out.

Cemented boles,
Rusted iron chains and poles
That prop
Her tattered Lears, Her bird-cage lime-trees up...

Under their branches, up and down
The beat now sacrosanct to dog with don
Once patrolled the Ladies of the Town....
As you carefully lean on the pox of the parapet
Think of the poet Collins taken for debt,
Exactly, historically, there, just under it,
Drunk in the afternoon....

Where Her false-gentle memory glides
Kissing smooth corners, (which are not),
Is roughly four yards from the spot
Where poor Colonel Windebanke,
For giving way to undue funk
At the sight of Ironsides,

One paint-fresh morning such as this
By some outraged friends of his
Was brought and shot....

No need to go on.
The Lady's gone.

A cow in the meadow blows her horn
Across the liquid green.
Were it not for milking time
No cow no grass no water-colour scene.
One meaning of our catalogue is that.

Lady, agreed this silence
Is solace. But You must confess the violence
Blending us together,
Past, present, future,
Calm beauty, rough weather.
Not one without the other.

Memo to Travellers

In this room where advertisements
At rare, sought-after moments
Drain of meaning – ideas and shops and overcoats,
Impedimenta of our grand mistake,
Take on the status of a public joke –
Here reality visits me and explains
The I that rots the middle of my dreams.
Naked, male and elegant
He traces with a nonchalant
Unhurried finger
Patterns of his news along my wall.
He comes and goes like a cat, my visitor,
Banishing fear with his gouging laughter.
While he is there I ask him,
'Shall I come near
The icy peaks you bask on, or shall I fall?'

He wipes the wall.
He hates my language.
'If not frost-bitten by pride
As you go.
What an end,' he laughs at me, 'to find
Nothing up there; no one coming after;
Truth like tuppence in your wasted hand.'

Oh
That laughter!

Sonnet

We endow our gods with wrath but never exasperation.
Which is why few ever hear their deity tetch:
'If they touch what they love they love what they touch
Not what they loved. Refrain from touching
Out of respect and they will love
Their abstaining selves, whatever their intention.
Thus it never remains as love was and they adduce
Triumphantly a theory of flux, of love
Sacred and profane. Ennobling love of God
Through an arbour relationship pungent with camphor,
Or Laura keeping a young man from himself,
Both fee-less educations of the heart.
May they guess sometime that love's not intended for gain;
Leave Us to judge what's sacred, what's profane.'

Niobe

Dropped from the bubble-blown womb in a mess to begin with,
I assumed the critical faculty like an inheritance
which it is not, I guess, watching the phalanx
of ambiguous treasons advancing, whose personal history
is identical to mine, and all the moments
of wetting my pillow with pure-as-possible grief
are rehearsed and repeated on different pillows
or sometimes on the same
but for casually different reasons
by those who betray me now –
whom my tears and my living betray.

Gardens are Lonely Places

Rain shall slake its dryness
   At the lips of trees.
Branches blow the wind back,
   Blossoms suck bees.
And so shall May trick always
   The acrobat and clown.
Who makes the world his circus
   Enjoys it upside-down.
Bare branches in the winter
   Dance in his rolling eye
A confident mime of growing
   Roots in the frozen sky.
Then persistence pierces the rockery,
   Patience erupts in the court,
Concrete cracks with abstractions
   Just as the acrobat thought.
So roses blow their trumpets,
   Shall fanfarron all day,
Knowing what their fate is,
   Are with reason gay.

They live by the bright reversion
   That hangs in the marquee sky,
While clowns inherit pennies,
   One for every eye.

A Refusal to Mourn Fashionably

Living by water the welshman sang,
life-drunken coon, of our humanity.
Swirling all ways his meanings bounced
like pebbles from the skull of commonplace.
Soon he took heart and died. His locks were lank
with rhetoric screamed back at starving gulls,
his face carved into chaos by defeat.

His noon-day death was almost understood.
Until public opinion and ashamed reviews
glutting like worms on, dead, his every mark,
continued to make his glorious non-success
a comfortable image; a fresh murder.

The Deep-sea Trends

*Like most of my contemporaries I pride myself on being
alert to trends.* – Marcus Cunliffe in ENCOUNTER.

*Major writers have always been the men who digested their
time, mastered its trends, and wrote in full consciousness
of them, the Platos, the Dantes, the Shaws.*
      – Colin Wilson in LONDON MAGAZINE.

Divers get me if they go too deep
But deep for them's not nearly deep enough
To understand which way the currents blow
Fish cities when the water's rough.
But still they dive because they wish to know

...Something. I respect their discontent.
And sometimes, if they're careful, let them down
To rise and tell the world what last year meant.
Some dive who do not worry if they drown,
In innocence they pass beyond my range
And if they surface do not take the town,
For who can lecture on a deep sea-change?

The Perky Traveller Ponders

The sea, like a band of elastic, snaps me back
Into my beach-hut and my sandy towel.
The coffin-accepting, traveller-drinking sea
Has two edges: a taut bow-string for a land-bound pellet, .
And a bed for a barque caring nothing for trade-wind or track,
Preciseness of consonant, niceness of vowel,
Least of all for location of next-day billet –
In short, a bed for nobody; not me,
However much I wish
To make a breeding pilgrimage, like fish.
I have no choice. For me one edge, not both.
And to know that should be enough
To prove the final irrelevance of the sea
To all but sailors.
                    I know on the other side
Live people no stronger or wiser or cleaner than I am.
Both here and there the here-and-there good is as rare.
So why should I suffer these feckless white horses to ride
My conscience like kobolds into the welcoming glisten?
The Sea, the Land and I have different voices. Listen.

'While Three Men Stand Together'

While three men stand together
The kingdoms are less by three
    – Swinburne

The time has come for us to say we're sorry:
That we never wore peaked hats, or stood
As candidates for conscience,
That we never
Entered the Prison or Colonial Service,
But left all that to ambitious professional men.
(As though we, the deplorers, were not ambitious
For ourselves and for the world we let others run.)
Those of our number who entered public life
Either changed – to our mean amusement –
Or came to grief in a strangely lonely way,
If you think of the number of us who were left on their side
When we last had a meal together
And joined in deriding the gospel of expedience.
But active dreamers we leave to die alone,
Or live, tight-lipped and contemptuous of our fine feelings,
Becoming, we tell each other, 'difficult',
Apt to make rude noises and leave the room
When the Talk gets going and Truth
Smells bitter-sweet in thin, balloon-shaped glasses.

The time has come for us to say we're sorry
To all the untimely dead, the unjustly accused.
To a groaning world we decided was past all order,
For every faith we watched become impure
And prided ourselves on stepping back in time,
Sorry for these and this, and how much more?

At a Public Rejoicing

I have done two years apprenticeship under
The man who tells the dirtiest stories south
Of the Humber. Three years I also laboured
With him who plays the castanets with his dentures.
Across the sea I served another two
For a tall man who imitates the songs of birds
On the violin: for I was told,
'If you can't laugh with us you're not with us.'
But I am with you. Oh! I am with you.
There is no one else but myself to be with.
My serving-time being over I am with you.
But I look up and when I believe it
You shall (I hope) yes you shall hear me
Truly laugh. Truly laugh.
For you, and with you.

The Words of Mercury to a Muse

Yes, I can sell you a song if you want me to.
Harsh and cold and almost gay like you.
Poets write poems to stop poetry,
They're not strong enough to bear it.
That you will never see.
No one has ever had any pain small enough for you to share it.
Poets write poems about their poems in case they die of fright.
Yes, if you want to, you can stay the night.
I shall lie over you like a dirty sheet,
Yet in your loss and my loss there's something sweet.
You, a progressive cow, content with counterfeit,
Me, emblazoned with losses and crosses like boils,
I scratch against your skin until you sleep
Smiling, Heaven, and everyone else, knows why.
Me not smiling. Nor do I weep;
It being impossible in your presence decently to cry.

Wherever I may go, it doesn't matter where to,
You could not follow.
Nor would you care to –
The words of Mercury are harsh after the songs of Apollo.

The Devil Speaking

'I think, you know,
That soon I shall write again.
I notice the pigeons down-pigeoning
In the dirty rain
As I roll on the surf of the crowd
Along Oxford street.
Don't you think it odd
(For I am split you know
Split where I cannot join),
Odd that a blow
One can suffer can be too great?
And, as I move along the street,
Has it, I ask myself, fallen,
Or is it yet to fall,
The thunderbolt, on that man,
Whose eyes are gone out,
Or rather, in,
Like cockroaches into cracks?
Is it the joy, or is it the pain he lacks?
The latter say I, for as you see
I live.
My hands move,
Flutter in front of your face.
Open the door,
Take your coat,
And, (if it's a very dull night)
I do not doubt,
Caress –
Without feeling.

So perhaps they might,
(There's no telling)
Write;
Also without.'

Visitation

Through screeching Mardi Gras figures, scorning a mask,
He bonily shouldered his way towards his task;
To where, remote, at the heart of the circling crowd,
Silent, for she was Silence, his love stood.
Snatched up in the dance sometimes, he was always thrown
Back to where he started from, alone.
Doggedly back he barged, he crept;
Never drew nearer; clung to a wall and wept.
He dreamed himself in profile on her snows,
Caught in his perfect, self-transcending pose.
He let his beard grow, and his eye grew in
Towards the rich confusion of his dream.
Then, quite suddenly, she came to him.
He hadn't expected that.
                              He ducked with fear.
She understood, and smiling, waited near.
Admonished by her smile, he too was still and saw
As in a magic paint-book shapes appear,
Limbs, voices, faces among the crowd,
Elegance of glance and attitude
He had been blind to. Thus she helped him learn
That to be lonely is only to be alone.
And so he asked of Silence, where she stood,
To fill his every-day with every good;
And gratefully watched his goddess, she whose lips
Were carved for sacred silence, over tea-cups,
Match curtains, ask him what she ought to wear.
No thing too small. All grew beneath her care
Exactly the size of itself, absent-mindedly loved
By one with no need for possessiveness, one who moved
Through other men's choices intact as an heir

To all answers. Caring and having no care
So precisely and simply is granted to only the pure
He knew, who lacked faith for good reason, and trembled for her.
But entered a world he remembered where all was sure
Today, and was, tomorrow, still more sure.
Then she left him.
                    Not for another face;
But silently glided back to her former place.
Left him alone with all he has to learn:
To see the maskers frenzy start up again,
Words flail with gesture, whether to curse or bless
Without her he can't hear, but knows like a caress
Her presence in the centre, standing still;
Relying on the cunning of his will
To make the journey this time back to her.
Her sureness of his strength is his despair.
He stares at the backs of the crowd and stares and tries
By prayer to speed the closing of his eyes.
And when her rebuke comes sighing round his ear,
He cries, to drown the chaos of that prayer.

ON THE WAY TO THE DEPOT

(1967)

Saint Tropez

Cast off in a boat without even a head for companion
You washed up here and I must say they gave you a welcome:
Renamed their gulf and their village and every so often
Fire guns at the ground in your honour.
You couldn't have known you'd so noisily float to the future
When someone in Pisa repeated
The claims of a dim jewish mystagogue thirty years hanged:
So what made you refuse to deny them
When Nero your master requested and thereby lose your head?
Those who back the wrong cult have to do without bangs
On their nameday. And it's hard, surely,
To lay down your neck for a long-shot, all alone?

Well, now you've a life-size painted porcelain portrait
Complete with moustache (a chocolate-coloured d'Artagnan)
A trellis of red paper flowers and, every day, roses.
An unthrifty aureole, even, of high-watt bulbs
Burns all day and night in the dark of your church.
Today the obedient carry your head in procession.

Teach us, Signore, to love a good thing when we see one:
Also the perfect moment to disobey.

16 May 1962

Dominus Illuminatio Mea

Ah! What creeping of late-summer shadows from the yew trees
Rooks' restlessness and evening gramophones...

We sped (you're as young as you feel)
From London in the roadster,
Opened the borrowed cottage, had us a fry-up,
Tossed a coin for the four-poster bedroom
And went to our separate dreams.

What a wonderful thing is male friendship!
You, planning a sure domestic murder
(Sexual freedom is an onerous thing
But love love love ah! love is King!)
I, (old friend of you both) required to lend
A confiding, tolerant ear for the week-end.
And now we're waiting for the pubs to open
Reading the Sunday papers in Trinity garden.
Spiked in the wall-top mortar, coldly, like emeralds, glow
Hand-slicing broken bottles drunk two centuries ago.

O barbered walks leading to bird-perch statues –
I follow where you lead!
Newman's head startles, impaled on a plinth,
As though he'd been executed and dipped in green.

The college cat
Is contentedly playing with something on the grass:
The squeak of living bones, alas! carries the distance.
Surely it's nearly seven!

Bartok is ribboning over a sill chipped clean
In the nick of its crumble away.
For a new generation?
Where will they put them all? Where will they put the cripples?
But we live, after all, and this was a place,
A week-end, good as another to miss the point in.

Lines for my Father

Methods of dodging are as many
As kinds of emptiness, and you were master
Of every kind and method.
Once in a decade unwillingly
Trapped in no laughing matter
You were curiously tender;
Otherwise brisk, and plump with contradictions:
Able to pray, even think, like a bigot, you'd argue

Some poor priest's ears red;
At times of partings you slipped away so aptly
To seek out crowds, as though they hid salvation;
A faithful, beloved husband, often drunk.
There seemed such strength of emotion in your evasions!
Above all there were jokes, and yours were good ones,
Indeed they fed and clothed us, paid my school.
Were you happy ever? Do you still snort at such questions?
When you stared at the wall when you died, what did you see?

Plain Tale from the Hills

They didn't like the colour of our skins
(not having time to discover our sympathies).
What the hell? We'd other sins
we'd got away with. There's a kind of justice.

Surprising, their hostility, how it shaped our lives.
Bien pensants, we were forced behind barbed-wire
which kept them out and us, effectively, in:
with Oil executives (the Firm sent home their wives)
who paid for quick release behind the Club
and called the girls black monkeys as they wiped their flies.

Frogs at night in the garden were the sound
of iron hooves in a courtyard echoing round and round;
the elastic snap of a tree-snake spoiled our noon.
If we opened the window (sick of the air-conditioner)
we let in the soft night-time murmur
from the squatters' leaf-huts, which shouldn't have been there
anyway, spoiling the avenue.

But we doted on Rex the Alsatian with his soft brown eyes,
gentle, affectionate – yes, old Rex was loyal! –
trained to go for the throat of any intruder.
And we loved the old house-boy till sensing a change of order
he started to keep the money on the empties.
Mildly rebuked for this (servants were scarcer)

being unused to dishonouer, and confused,
he went to the master-bedroom, sat on the bed and slipped his
knife in his groin and pulled it up to his navel.
It was Rex's whimpers of pleasure attracted us,
lapping the blood that trickled down the hall.

The Spring

(Korea 1951)

The paper house was empty in the middle of the paddy
So we took it over. The electricians
Fixed up some wiring; we had a crate of
Guinness in the lorry; we'd come a long way
But first we must get settled.
The partitions, the rooms, were small. The locals were small,
But the owner must have been a man of some substance,
There were plenty of rooms, and the house miles from nowhere.
Soon there were yellow bulbs swinging from black flex;
All had their quarters; a dry-patch for the lorries...
Then somebody smelled the burning.
Something wrong with the wiring.
Up to our anklets in mud
We watched it burn down, drinking Guinness.
Nothing for it now but put up tents on the dry-patch.
A man floated face downward in the mud.
There were helmets and webbing equipment we didn't
Inquire under. Now there was kerosene
In the tents, and wooden duck-walks.

In front of the smouldering house,
In the shallow pond where the man lay,
Was a bubble of spring; in the morning
We went there to wash. It was warm.
Out of the earth, dribbling on to the mud
Between two stones, came a spring that was warm.
We used it to shave in; while around,
Women patiently gathered with their washing:
The people whose blessing it was
Waiting for us to go.

August by the River

Hunched-up, muttering along the *quais*
Of deserted, bus-ticket-blown SW3,
After one too many a *table d'hôte* meal
Eaten alone with a book, I think of Jules
Laforgue. As I zig-zag along beside
The only river that openly solicits suicide,
I think of St Barnabas, Addison Road,
Only a couple of postal districts away
Where, oddly enough, he married a Miss Leah Lee.
With my pockets stuffed full like confetti with telephone
Numbers I'll never ring up, I stop to stare the moon
Over Battersea full in its diesel-fumed eye,
For I'm terrified stiff of the quiet in my *chambre meublée*.
Why do I think of Jules Laforgue and his bride?
Because by this stretch of the river, whose arms
Offer their piss-yellow, typhus-ridden charms –
Because it's probably wiser and safer in this *quartier*
To think of them and not of you, or me.

Watch this Space

When they placed in position de Witter's 'Adam and Eve'
On the front of the Marriage Counsel Office block –
Two low-relief panels with a space between,
Two oblong verticals, asymmetrical – the shock
They gave us was (presumably)
Something to do with his cock
And her petals. Both showed, certainly.
But even after they'd been taken down
And his knocked off and hers smoothed in
Their modified presences still disturbed our town.
What is it about them? We don't believe
In this of course, but isn't it odd
That in the uncarved space between the figures, some god,
Some kind of superstition appears to stand
Guarding a silence with an empty hand?

Wherever You Are

Dropped fully grown, conceived by autogenesis,
My smiling devils are gaolers who simulate friendliness
The better to break me. They thrive in the semi-awake
Of the utterly dark of their birth-place. One, arm around my neck,
Explaining why I keep my curtains drawn:
'Why bother to open them? When you look down
I am all the faces of the town.
Be honest now: when did you last see a different one?'
His birth and his chatter exhaust me. For peace I lie down and confess
My god is theirs whose name is nothingness.

But in our darkness the warm-lipped angels also have their places,
More terrible by far,
Whose wings are wands of anamnesis,
More than flesh and blood and brain can bear.
My devils are easier, teaching forgetfulness!
But if I turn away
From these insupportable angels of memory
I pull a blind of horror between me
And the natural world: pig-snout and bird-claw instead of hands and
    faces.

You must save me angels! Tell me what to do!
'Action is all the meaning left you now.
Lift up your back from the bed,
Strain till the sweat is running down your head
To repeat like a parrot what we tell you to say:
I believe in you, angels. Devils, you lie.'

And now on the screen of myself, in the dark I can see
Each watchful face that, hurt, like all ours are,
Opened like a child's face, like a flower,
While it was looking at her.

Theirs than hers are easier to remember.

Quickly now . . . what phrases can I mutter,
Having reached this far, to weave them like a charm
Round the legs of my bed

Before the dark in me begins to swarm
And puts out all the daylight from my head?
How sweeten my tongue? How summon the flavour of her?

Now, as prisoners rotting in the black
Of forgotten dungeons pick from stinking straw
Their half-dry faeces, using them as chalks to draw
Crucifixions, a flower, a beloved name, in the dark,
So I use this, my day-long, night-long back-
And-forth to scratch your name with.
                                    You, the law
I live by, in the dark. You, the tenement
By rarest, luckiest accident,
Of more than you knew, more than your mirror saw.

And so in the dark I talk to you out loud.
I no longer know if I talk to you or God.

And what have you to do with prisoners and darkness,
Black and white angels, metaphors of pain,
Whose soul was so strong it retained that initial, mysterious happiness
The rest of us lose at once, and never have again?
You are the silence I listen to,
The landscape of the dark I move through –
And none of these things –
                            the dark is mine
And yours and ours – oh help me see
How all the angels in the darkness can agree
That nothing I have, not even my pain is my own:
That under an absence like a stone, I must be gay!

Westwell Churchyard, Oxfordshire

Sky mother-of-pearl. Oyster-colour sun
A furry lemon,
Silent, full of silences.
Birdless windless trees hold breath;
Stream tinkles to pond to be frozen to death.

Silence: a hand clapped over a mouth;
Violent, with suppressed violences.
Earth is preoccupied, waiting to know
The soft grope of snow.
Muscles of a bough crack, pistol-shot, echo echo...
On a little mound
Near stream, by pond,
A church: a square of yellow stone,
Some of it ferried over seas from Caen
In boats too light, you would have thought,
To bear the weight,
Ages of faith ago.
Moss on the church-yard gate.
Green grass prickles the hoar-frost sheet.
And then the moment like a film-shot freezes.
Perceived, not seen, almost out of frame:
Joy. A presence,
Transforming all the other presences:
And leaning against your new-cut yellow stone
A splash of carmine
A scatter of frozen
Bokhara roses...
And then the blur of snow. Time to be gone.

Sequence

New Year's morning
    I didn't love you, you didn't love me,
    you stayed for no reason but soft attraction
    and snow on the road to North London.
    You were large and beautiful and jewish
    and very warm. We slept
    unsatisfied each, and quite content.
    And when in the morning you stood in the light
    slowly to strap your daytime on
    was born in me the power to love again.
    Simple as that.
    And you, thank God in love with somebody else

(such moments are not rushed upon so soon)
laughed in the mirror with wonder – Look
I've last year's make-up on!
And you were gone.

January
>Beauty's a flame
>draws us on and on.
>A candle inside a hollow, sculpted head.
>Huddled head to head
>we kept our mysteries all afternoon.
>No one is anything now. If you leave
>collapsed on my table, your hand's covering, your glove,
>empty of fingers, full of bought fragrance – if I move
>to hold it for a moment to my face
>I know I yearn
>not wholly for you:
>but once again
>according to the law we serve
>I want to burn.

February
>Leaning on Waterloo Bridge after ninety days
>of dark and snow and sludge in sudden sun:
>there are black-headed gulls all round *Discovery*;
>there's Blackfriars and Westminster and out-of-sight Lambeth
>and concave pencilling skyscraping Vickers
>(unfinished) and altogether a sense of bank-to-bankness,
>of being near a river in a city.
>Buying an evening paper at two o'clock
>among the girlie books the breasts
>and buttocks and (curious taste) suspenders,
>I blame myself for being so lost in myself
>I have to remember the miracle blue of the sky
>and to bless the man who coloured buses red.
>(There are still the letters PLEASURE GARDEN
>clinging to a mass of cemented rubble).
>I'd like to palp the typists as they pass.
>For I am happy.
>What else can you be when two
>enormous out-of-scale hetaerae hold up
>the portico of a station called Waterloo?

51

April

I have a fear we shall quarrel
when we are alone.
You, opinionated foolish, beautiful,
who all the virtues own
of the over-demanding, over-fastidious mind.
Who live without a friend
save the man you love, and me.
How shall the red fox, flushed from the roots of his tree,
wagging his red brush, playing at dog,
nose tender with hedgehog,
and you, lover of uncornered foxes, ever agree?
Well, says the red fox, wait; wait and see.

June

Phrases out of a letter:
'Running elbow to elbow with the President's brother
in the three-legged race his long-legged daughters
had huge, dark eyes.'
Does it matter?
So many girls in the world.
Who will bother?
Stripped, heads shaven, one in line with the other,
could we, as a uniformed guard, three weeks after
going on oven-duty
guarantee
even to raise a flicker?

My hands hang down, stream blood.
I cannot distinguish.
The crowd
is over me like a hood of blood.

On the plate of a body bearing a head
someone has carried this letter, watches me read it.
Odd
to distinguish a head in Horrible Town
and it still on.

Now I'm a bird and looking down:
white distempered in a believable sun
a place for people

is built on Horrible Town;
almost
almost bearing it down.

Cold light of the moon, over the sleeping sea,
over the whale-back islands, over me
here in a cottage on the mountain's hip,
capture me, asleep.
Drag my memories through your freezing streams
until they're come out cold and hard as stones
I can hold in my hand:
stones I can build with,
the dreams and memories my waking days are filled with.
I want a stone tower made of them in my mind;
one I can climb, and signal from, and understand.

On the Way to the Depot

It's a pleasant night. So tonight I'll talk on the way
Of the images I seem to think in every day
Five strange years after:
Of how my life appears to me.
I don't speak of it, the thing itself, not that,
But of how I seem to see our lives in the light of it.
It's as though you live in big rooms filled with laughing;
I see little tables, and shining black pianos,
And you very busy. And me outside in the street
(Don't laugh) sweeping it.
The place I suppose is my idea of heaven.
I haven't described it (who could?)
But I've put in some writing desks and black pianos
Because that's, if I'm honest, the best my poor brain can rise to
Without inventing. Spirits, like flames that meet
Melting into each other – yes, that makes sense to me often
But not (and you know this) every day...
Anyway, here I am
Out on the pavement. And every night

53

I wheel my day's collection to the depot
Where it's assessed. But
(And here's the odd part)
I don't know who does the assessing
Or what it's best to bring. One just leaves it all there
And goes to bed; every day.
The streets and dreams and faces that I've seen now
Without you. Or with you?
     It's late.
Time to turn in my collection.
Heaven knows how I'm doing!
When I sleep
Visit me then, reassure me. Don't share my puzzle.
And let me hear you laugh at my dustman's hat....

Afternoon in Sneem

At three o'clock on the green
a Vauxhall stops and out of the boot
in a resonant unaccompanied baritone comes
Christ crucified for me.
None of the lips move of the men who are in it.
The fairground men from Ballylongford
lean on their hammers;
children out of school, their plastic sandals
hanging in their fingers, wait to listen;
and the men under the eaves
or inside M.J. O'Sullivan's, Riney's, P.J. Burns',
their hillsides left to the wet,
stare at their boot-toes.
'We are not Jehovah Witnesses.'
Boot-lid lifted, tape-recorder switched
to crowd-speaker, a pale, stout young man
in a broad tie and a tie-clip: 'We disagree
with all their teachings.'

'They're Jehovah's Witnesses.' Huge hat tipped back,
the village doctor, venal sheriff out of a Western,
loudly pronounces. 'They all believe
they're saved. It comes from America.'
'That sounds easy' says the friendly visitor.
'I find *my* religion easy.' Chin thrust out;
uncontradicted, champion of the Church, rolls to the pub next door.
The pints all sigh, relax their gaze
fixed over glass-brim, nowhere.
'There's nothing wrong in what they're saying'
whispers a cap, 'they're Christians anyway.'

Old Jack Mountain, half in half out,
his ears holding his hat up, is caught.
'Are you saved?'
                  'We'll see now.'
'Then don't you trust in the Lord?'
'Now I never said that.'
'Good theology' nods a listening trilby.

Outside the rain is falling in hatfuls.
Dowager Winnie behind the bar
absently dusts a loaf, rolls up some twine,
combs the froth off the stout-jug
and peers through her peephole across the empty green.
The Ballylongford men are taking their ease in doorways –
Dance till ten to the Fabulous Des O'Donovan and his Five
Sisters (Galway) – their half-up Bingo tent is sagging water,
peeling roundabout horses tilt in mud.
'I read in a book' comes from the empties corner
'written in America,
that weather will make this country
unfit for habitation.' Takes a sip:
'They didn't put a date on it.'
'Trouble was' (Jack, judicially, over a second)
'I never had a long enough read at the Bible.'

Outside on the green in the Vauxhall the four city-men
pent in by bruise-coloured mountains,
sit staring in silence before them
their windows slowly misting in the rain.

The Temperance Billiards Rooms

The Temperance Billiards Rooms in red and green and brown
with porridge-coloured stucco in between
and half a child's top for a dome, also green –
it's like a Protestant mosque! It'll come down;
no room for this on the Supermarket scene.
Eight years ago on a Saturday afternoon
we used to walk past it, for no particular reason,
dressed in our weekend clothes now long out of fashion,
and bump into friends, newly married, just as we were,
and go to a film, or not, or window-shop.
Eight years before that I was seventeen,
eight years from now I may be forty-one;
thirty-three salutes the Billiards Rooms alone.
Because I'm the one who's alive still, but without much enthusiasm,
for loving someone has no particular season,
just goes on, as I do too I notice; not only from fear –
though it's true I don't want to go for I've never been there –
but while you are breathing it takes a decision to stop;
and I'm vaguely pleased to see that green and brown
(something so uneconomical's sure to come down)
in all its uselessness waiting out its season:
pleased to find the Temperance Billiards Rooms still here,
and for all I know men playing billiards temperately in there.

In the Rubber Dinghy

In the rubber dinghy on the lake
watched from the bank I secretly touched your leg
when I should have been watching you.
You were pleased but it was the wrong thing to do.
I was afraid and it was a trick
like watching a star askew;
stare straight at it and you miss the glow.
I protected myself and I protected you.
We touched as lovers do

pretending to paddle the boat on the little lake
when my whole life was burning for your sake;
watched from the bank by others whose treasure you were
but who didn't love you as I did and could stare
safely straight at you and marvel at what they saw.
You were mine because you'd decided so.
For safety I did as other lovers do
when that wasn't what was needed then. No.
We could have fallen together into the glow
that was waiting. I wanted a slow
lifetime for that and looked askew.
So we were simply happy and laughed on the lake
and I have a lifetime to think out my mistake.

Perfection Isn't Like a Perfect Story

I think often of the time I was perfectly happy.
And sat by the harbour reading a borrowed Cavafy.
You were with me of course and the night before we
Played bar billiards, green under lights, in the café
Postponing our first shared bedtime and every ball
That didn't come back made us look at each other and down.
I collected the key and we crossed the late-night hall
And seeing the room you cried, it was so small.

We were too close. We bore each other down.
I changed the room and we found that you were ill.
Nothing was perfect, or as it should have been.
I lay by your side and watched the green of dawn
Climb over our bodies and bring out of darkness the one
Perfect face that made nothing else matter at all.

Not Being a Man of Action

Lenin in Zurich given burnt porridge by his landlady:
'How lucky we are to have roast every day!'
Laughed, and went back to the Public Library;
dreams of action nourishing his exile.

A cottage in the middle of the wood.
Pipe and fire both drawing well;
even a glass of Teacher's whisky at my el-
bow...
Danton, Castro...
Men of action cannot flinch at blood.
I can though.

I know a company director who says
he'd kill anybody, he'll be bought
for a hundred thousand if he can't be caught.
He has the courage of our logic, which is money.
Whereas
the citizens of Rostov are very proud of
their new theatre
built in the shape of a tractor.
Each finds the other dangerous, and funny.

The kingcups burn like gas-jets by the lake.
Just before dark
blackcaps sang berserk behind the cottage.
At times, when I'm awake,
not half-asleep,
I'd like to go swimming, swimming, swimming in that lake,
but it's muddy, and nowhere more than three inches deep.

The delicate deer flick see-saw by to hide.
Up on the road at the top the huntsmen ride –
today the Hunt –
each heavily straddles his expense-account.

I live in this wood, like a marvellous green cage.
The bars are stationary, like trees:
outside are the slipping fields; I can go where I please.

O adder at my feet, your head
the size of my little finger-nail,
today I had to tread
on your neck, small as a cuticle,
watched your belly turn the colour of gun-metal.
O birds O flowers O snakes O fire-in-the-belly oatmeal
O Nelson cigarettes O Teacher's whisky
O daily daily daily
Daily Mail!
Killing hardly anything
I assert my triumphant uselessness, and sing,
while the auditioning stars on their cold blue xylophone go ting! ting!
    ting!

Satire I
(after Sir Thomas Wyatt)

for Patrick Creagh

My own John Patrick, since you'd like to know
    why did I leave my rich place at the court,
    or the nowadays version of it, where men go
(and you'd go too if asked, and so we ought)
    to make some money and to make a name
    innocently seeking to be sought
among the Wits, the Expenses and the Fame –
    I'll tell you what I know, as Wyatt told
    his friend John Poynz he'd given up the game,
gone back to Kent and Christendome and cold.
    Though Wyatt had a convention. He could say
    he didn't want their places and their gold,
not if his conscience was the price to pay;
    could leave out private reasons and moralise
    in the Palace versus Pastoral of his day.
While we, JP, are too well taught the lies
    our super-ego tells us, to be sure
    quite what we're up to in our ego's eyes.
He knew this too of course, and knew the lure
    towards the chandeliers for the poet-moth,

who wakes one day to find he can't endure
the trail of his monologue or the drone of his sloth
   one strophe longer, nor his fear he may
   have lost his sense and self-respect and both
will never cohabit again. He has to see
   if he exists at all outside his head
   (he knows he does some of the time, but you'll agree,
while living – it's sometimes splendid when he's dead –
   a poet's a burdensome, touchy thing to be).
   He goes there needing praises, love and bread
in just that order alas, and spoils all three
   by dragging with him the old chain and ball
   of his nagging other self: You think you're free
to take up masks and drop them: what if all
   your careful evasions, your meaningful standings-apart
   never meant anything but your own withdrawal?
Others commit their faces; you, by bat-light,
   a shadow at the window, *watch* the game.
   The sap in trees falls down as you recite
the one thousand variations on your name. –
   You see, John Patrick? I'm telling you why I went
   whereas Wyatt could take that for granted; but he'd the same
reasons I'm certain: a secular discontent
   with his divine one, and the brief illusion
   of a life more 'real' in London than in Kent.
You'll say the parallel's false, that television
   isn't today's equivalent of the court.
   'Your head's still on' you say. But the admiration,
the power, the cutting-a-figure-ness, the short
   shrift for those who weaken, the same nice
   distinctions between half-lies by men half-bought
that asken helpe of colours of devise
   to joyne the mene with eche extremitie,
   with the nerest vertue to cloke always the vise
(and thereby trivialise disastrously:)
   these not-quite-crooks, who care, and that's the worst
   I cannot, I. No, no, it will not be.
And not much to be proud of: at the first
   whiff of a compromise to up sticks and away
   hasn't much glamour about it, suggests a thirst
to be safer than sorry that we might call today
   by a harsher name, perhaps, than Wyatt knew.

But I'll not bother to find one, though it may,
like nearly everything else, be nearly true.
So many lives to live – so little time.
Look – in these woods I've leisure to write to you.

Though…what's the use if I should learn to climb
into a still attention and my eyes
go blunt as fingers pushing at old green
backdrops hung on hooks from plaster skies?
This lake has less to offer than a bar.
There isn't any point in telling lies
(you'd find me out if I did): these trees are far
from substitute religion. Why pretend
that most of the time they say much? But they are
(I watch them, as I write this, sway and bend,
these beeches, their powdery trunks, less than half-way –
this valley's, you know it, a hole under the wind,
it seldom reaches here – and the beeches' sway
wastes itself at the top, the bole is still)
they are – what? Presences? Undemanding? They
obscurely help me. Or perhaps they will.
Pink buds begin, which seems a hopeful sign…
I am such an ordinary fool.

There's Pearse – *in Spaigne where oon must him inclyne*
rather than to be, owtewerdly to seme:
he shares our darkness, lights it up with wine;
let him who risks it be the first to blame.
Fear of life – is that it? Shall we ever
see proved our belief it's the opposite, learn to name
what swirls our darkness like a fish, the bright diver
the under-sea mover in the imagination?
Will it surface today, tomorrow (we're watching) and give a
hard, fast reason for a long obsession?
So many lives to live, and none for long:
times for watching, feeling for salvation.
Or will that fish by leaping prove us wrong,
and fall back limply, by its fall convey
there's only dark, and that's where fish belong?

Pearse, and you *where Christ is given in pray*
for mony, poison and traison in Rome

(only the method improved since Wyatt's day)
and I (for a while) in Gloucestershire, at home,
    eating court-earnings, bored with terza rhyme;
    where if thou list, John Patrick, *for to come*
thou shalt be judge how I do spend my time.

Diptyque touristique

1

The languorous isles, the tall bright-green bamboo;
the part of the plage where the girls run about toute nue
and the men oil themselves standing up hoping you're looking;
the helicopter at three o'clock, making
sure you're not doing whatever it is you're not meant to be doing.
The blackened young man dons his necklace and black chiffon shirt
and crimson trousers cut so tight they hurt.

The old girl with a young one at each horned foot scraping
and another two at her frizz of hair de-crêping
while she bulges, split apart, in her swimming suit:
the Salon de beauté, nine o'clock at night.

Every morning in the chic hotels
unsunburnt girls rinse out the lavatory bowls.
This is the perfect place, the perfect light;
Only for the altogether perfect could the price be right.

2

I resent having feet.
His feet, my feet, their feet; everyone has feet:
Feet – what a word! – all white
with shoes and crumpled up and useless.
If it was wings now...ah!
But perhaps there'd be hair under them;
and when I lifted them up
those around would receive the impression
also of how limited and ingloriously mortal
was the nature of my flight.

Goldie *sapiens*

When Goldie the golden eagle escaped from the Zoo
All the world went to Regents Park and we went too.
There he was, with an air of depression, a sooty hunch,
Digesting the grey-eyed merganser he had for lunch.
Under him children and coppers and mothers and fathers
And bare-kneed ornithologists with cameras
Hanging down to their ankles and lovers and others
Peeling damp cellophane from sandwiches stand and wait.
While running around in sad moustaches Keepers,
Hopelessly, like H.M. Bateman characters,
Shoo Pekes away from buckets of eagle bait.
Really, this bird was a National Occasion!
The Evening Standard published ah hourly bulletin
As though it was getting in training for Sir Winston.
And none of us knew what we most wanted to see,
The Keepers allowed to go home or the bird to go free.
There was an appalling sense of a happy ending too –
Goldie was free but he kept an eye cocked on his Zoo.
Just then there started up where Goldie was,
A thrush fit to burst but we didn't listen because
We were enjoying the sight we'd come to see –
The only free eagle in captivity.
Later that evening the Nation breathed a sigh.
Goldie like us, Goldie the human and sage,
With tail between talons, had lallopped back to the cage.

May

Road-menders are flowers today, blooming in jeans,
Are men in the smoking advertisements, lolling in bright machines
That drip black shining tongues along the lanes
Shaded-in after with sweet white watered stones.
Beeches' leaves are fresh today, are peeled grapes stuck
On barbecue branches; bluebells broken on the deer-track
Hang in a thin blue vertigo after the deers' night-time feet;
    And May is behaving again, in the colours appropriate.

Though since the first summer that opened us something in May
Is delivered like milk and papers for someone who's gone away,
What's gone from us isn't May's fault and isn't our business.
Whatever we've left is ours and all there is:
As summer is, and so are we (for this one) who salute
Those rafts of other Mays drifting out of sight,
Road-menders and the roads they mend and deers' blue feet
  Dripping dead flowers out in the dark tonight.

No One

  No one;
Only water, last year's leaves
  And this year's, newly grown.

  Walking alone.
Stumbling rather, through wet leaves
  And fallen branches and marshes

  Screened by beeches.
Following you, for why should you
  Not be ahead of me here

  As everywhere else you are?
No sounds; only the swish of my overcoat and water.
  Nothing among the sunless stream-bed flora

  Except a white-bibbed dipper
On a dripping branch
  Ten feet away

  Looking at me.
We both stand still, my nerve cracks first, I move,
  The bird moves further.

  Or rather
It guards the distance, keeping
  The string between us taut.

And if I caught
Up with the bird what would I do with it?
  Compress it like a silk scarf in my fist

  And then, like silk released,
Explode it back to the air.
  Graveyard bluebells, water, bird and me.

  Still I can see
No sign of you who must have gone
  (You always do) the other way.

Deathday

The doctor in his surgery
tells the patient to undress
and fumbling with his underdrawers
rapes the patient quickly.
He's seen enough of faces
going blue before they're wheeled away
to know to catch the flesh still warm,
his and theirs, you have to hurry.
That accomplished, at his table,
under the shaded table lamp,
approves the moisture of his fingers' ends,
sighs and from the hat-rack takes his hat
to feel its roundness rounding round his head,
to walk down shine-green corridors of sweat
he runs his fingers through –
always physical, absent-minded, leaving his mark.
Outside, the early editions of people and papers
go soggy in air, go glup and glup
down gratings, irretrievably over.
While, everywhere, hidden, in surprising places,
are those who from the inside of their heads
have hanging on a string a pendulum
that swings tick-tock, and never hurries.
Their eyes are deep as skies, go down

to the connected place – their faces,
carved like soap-stone, stem the waters.
These under oxygen when they die
are loud as radios as they're wheeled away.
These, with a stone's
patience, who have waited out
their drying season.

What is surprising is that not everyone's
only ambition in the world is
to be like them, and to love their tired eyes.

Closing down

(for K.K.)

Sometimes my whole being
    itches like a bird-table
lousy with starlings.

You itched all over.
    I would say 'Keep still'
myself jumping like a cracker.

How we got like that I do not know.
    You, Dionysus,
casting me for Apollo.

Me, posing as the settled one.
    You, married and three children;
puzzled by this.

So we fought;
    a blurted duologue of itching;
sharing that.

But you were an actor resenting the part he is given.
You only half-learned yours; and always
answered a door you didn't approve of and who

the hell dared knock at it anyway – *'You?'*
To understand, (I understood, as in a mirror)
is to forgive... some things. Not enough.
My only, and entirely, my brother.

Sometimes when I drove away
I saw you in the mirror
watching after me
standing in the street.
If I'd have turned
you would have feigned
indifference like a cat.

Coughing up cigarette butts
like gall-stones
drinking quick ones
quicker, pulling fast ones
faster, loss of self-respect
you had the courage
to acknowledge.
Even your self-pity
crocodile tears.
So, in the middle years,
although of course defeated
you were never gelded
by the city.

You were too human
to be good and too
good for your own.
And though it is true we never
talked perfectly or well
because I live I still
call on a wave-band
pitched only for you
which only you could hear;
each, in dumbness, the other.

Now no one hears a sound.
My only, and entirely my brother.

'This philosophy'
　　said Goethe,
'if what the Englishman tells us
　　is true,
has nothing foreign;
　　on the contrary,
the epochs through which we all pass
　　are repeated in it.
When we are children
　　we are sensualists;
idealists when we love,
　　and attribute
to the beloved object
　　qualities which she does not
naturally possess.'
　　(She might though, mightn't she,
naturally?)
　　'Love wavers,'
(it does, yes)
　　'we doubt her fidelity'
(the truth of our mutual feelings)
　　'and are sceptics
before we think of it.
　　The rest of life is indifferent;
we let it go as it will,
　　and end,'
(so that's it,
　　so that's what's coming on!
But, dear Heaven, he was nearly eighty!)
　　'like the Indian
philosopher, in quietism.'

Birthday

It's raining today, a dark rain,
On water and breaking trees. It's cold.
A day for dying and answering questions on.
Only a few dark days like this
I'm half-way through, I'm thirty-five years old.

And if I should die this minute – supposing –
Looking at nothing much, the wall
Between me, the lamp, and the coughing hillside,
How surprised would I be to snap off
Like a twig and go suddenly flying? Hardly at all.

You? With all your sins
Sticking like merde in your hair? And everyone
(Think how many you know already)
Who's got there before you waving like mad
And calling hallo like a wartime railway station?

Something like that. At least for a while.
Things fall away. We might go on –
Speak in a language of poppies and roses
With faces we love. There may be one
Or two we knew as deep as that, or one –

Who takes us and teaches us, and after,
So mixed up together we no longer care
Which is ourself or the other, go flying
As free and as one as a light flash, the fusion
Quick or as long, as irrelevant as a light-year.

It's pretty scary. But what is a soul
If not a big wish in a small fool
If we have one at all? One or two things
Suggest we may. But no more than you
Can I tell today if yesterday's message was true.

And not all of us soon, and none of us surely
Make for the light. It may depend
How thick our eyes go blind in the dazzle
After how deep and dark we dug
A frozen hole we fell through in the end.

The walls are shaking...The wind like an Irish
Country portent laughs in the rigging
Of coffin trees pretending it's crying.
Only a few dark days like this
To think how to climb from the hole these days are digging.

Surviving

I am oh, I am sick
oh, heartily, I am sick of grief
that's round me like a collar on a thief,
bending my neck
into an angle, wounded, weak,
an impermissibly apologetic back.

I count the towels we shared. They wear.
Burn them. Move on. Move on where?
Move on as usual, wearing the new collar?
('Rag and bone' a street man calls outside the cellar
where your dresses are...No one survives.
You are not the first of my two wives.

Time is not sequence.) Could I incorporate
our grief (no one ever has, we shriek
and bend the neck or turn our back
or die) if I could learn to bear
grief (and not the stupid collar that I wear)
then might we, both together, celebrate.

And Odysseus Wept

Pink nightdresses in pink, night, boutique windows
And every sweet elegant dream such things give rise to –
Why should I hate them, I've not been deprived of them?

Soft murmurs of terraces, lime trees and lapping of water;
Slim-ankled Ino, her eyes in the lamplight like water.
Why did they look at me, who had never dared pray for them?

The pride of attractiveness burns inside their faces,
Those who wear like togas their successes.
Why should I envy them, who have also won them?

Apartments where all is clarity – bathrooms smell
Of powdered skin, and sponges, and Chanel –
Why should I scoff, I who have thanked God for them?

The truth of love, perfections, visions, dreams,
A face in the morning, joy falling like coins –
Why should I bark at these, I who have counted them?

I, with the heart of a lover, heart of a hater,
Who have taken nothing easy since the day I was born,
Why should I hate the things I've taken, who have paid for them?

The girl in the bar who asks for a table for one,
A little crazy perhaps, but lovely, her hair hanging down,
Bypasses me and sits (I'm exact) with a cross-eyed Italian.

I don't even mind she misses out me, perhaps I prefer to watch them?
I have lived in the waves of the sea, tossed up, borne down.
Why should I weep at the waves, that have saved me and wrecked me
    so often?

Piazza di Spagna

Moving

There is a perfect
socket at the centre
in whose groove
our lives would move
                        effortlessly.
Some physical men
have sometimes found it;
great games-players
on their day:
Garfield Sobers;
what do the others
find so difficult?
See, his simpleness!

In happiness
I spread my arms.
Dark
fish move in their shadow.

And I rejoice
my life as it should be –
moving towards
                        effortfully
its centre –
a kind of
happy nightmare.

1966

ABOUT TIME

(1970)

Those whispers just as you have fallen or are
falling asleep – what are they, and whence?

COLERIDGE

One

My father barely believed in the private life.
His cronies were public, at home he mostly slept.
Even his death was in public, nurses wept
Intoning Catholic responses, and the worst
Was that his genuine public smile went first.

During the war, bombed from flat to flat,
My father's religious maxim – 'Travel Light':
Six months I oiled, then left behind, an unused cricket bat.
Up on the rack went the lived-out-of suitcases;
Below them the carriage rocked, like a breastful of medals, with faces.

A reaction to this is a longing to settle. Not down –
For a place to stay as it was till you return.
A room, a patrolling area, sufficiently your own
To give the illusion of white, vegetable, roots.
But my father's example put green nettles in my boots.

He was right, he was wrong, he was weak, he was strong,
Seeing the funny side (the dog it was that died):
Life – a show on the road, a series of one-night stands:
Doubt – a poison in the colon or an irritation in the glands:
The greatest sin – to spend life sitting on your hands.

No room for windy pretensions, his world was a vast
Gillray cartoon (only kinder), himself as absurd as the rest,
And private matters were not got off, but held close to, the chest.
What would you make of me now, mulling a personal past
In public, and in this quiet corner at last?

What would you make of this place? I do not know
And it's too late to matter. So many ways to slow
The spinning world. To move is one. Like mine your vertigo
Needed a balancing pole. But Prospero
Stuck-up on his island with his wand, and Trinculo

Burping in braces, headed for the bar,
Are not so far apart as they appear.
You, preferring donkey-rides at Margate, I prefer
(If you wish) this snobbish separation, like it here
Down eighty muddy steps and miles from nowhere

Travelling Light, in four walls, by a lake
Not even the Green Dragon locals know is here.
No electric light, water from fronded rock
Tasting of caves; food and fuel humped down on the back,
And the few planted flowers nightly eaten by deer.

And this place is an island. Round its shore
Predictable tides slap and suck with drear
Solipsist self-accusations, trying to drag me elsewhere.
Freud, it seems, was right: becoming your own master
You destroy The Father, shovel a way clear

For guilts to multiply like rabbits only faster.
Oedipus-like you mislike the joy of your eyes
In their sudden unfettered seeing – which may be Greek,
Tragic, Freudian, but is also lies.
I didn't come to hide, I came to seek.

First time down the steps we were stopped by a blast
Of orange and flame trombones (last year's beech leaves, beech-mast,
Undisturbed by the winds of a year and the rains
Because of the steep of the bank and intertwines
Of the beech-boughs) – this was a place, at last!

As orange trombones blared at us over yew-green
Water under a steady smoke-blue line
Of warm, eye-level mist beaded with black birds, and, brown,
The last of this year's leaves see-saw'd singly down
Like notes from a musical stave in a film cartoon –

A stone shed in a wood. A place of regraspable fact.
Our lives in the cities seem to become as abstract
As other people's pain on television. We barely meet and never give
More than we can afford. We sleep, and dream we live
Down streets through which enormous horrors move

Smiling like aunts...Who has never stood in Piccadilly,
Alone, watching the neon time unreel,
And felt more scared, trying not to be silly,
Felt more desolation than a man should feel
Drop like lead and overturn his belly?

...You keep me to doggerel, rightly, my Margate-
Preferring father. I hear you sniff and say,
Caring no more for the poet maudit
(Pronounce it to rhyme with 'audit') even than I
'Love in a Cottage' for those who can afford it!

Right! But listen to nightsticks of cowparsley quelling a riot
Of lesser herbage. Night and day, winter and summer, listen
In curious shadow, between two oil-lamps, to the quiet
(The sun, we are shadowed by forest, seldom prolongs a visit)
Of the waterfall, like a constantly flushing cistern.

Even if you saw the point (and you might)
Two days of dripping eaves in bottle-green light
And you'd puff, fast, to a bus-stop, to the lights across the park,
This is love-in-a-cottage all right.
It's starting again, travelling light, in dark.

Hogweed, horsetails, couch-grass, light-starved clematis,
Coal-tits, herons, moorhens, slow-worms – are dramatis
Personae of a mortality play. They make it clear,
Although we seem the star parts, one move from us
Of inattention or condescension and we disappear,

Just stand about looking foolish, looking at nothing,
At trees like green things in the way,
At defined tones of green turned to indefinite grey,
At worlds like Victorian servants doing whatever they're doing,
Kneeling, backs towards us, going away

To leave us, slumped, alone. These things are there.
And whether we are or not they neither know nor care.
To see them is – to see them (I thought moorhens were
Just black, they're different browns and fawns under a sheen)
Is a gift you can lose as though it had never been.

Is a gift...Just now I went to the wood to pee.
I'd forgotten the night. The night fell on my face
With a swift, dropping, dark, cold embrace.
An open-mouthed wind, a black, breathing tree,
The moon, the clouds, the muscled boughs were over me

And settled on my shoulders. The heavy night,
Cold as water, dark as a fish, offered me its weight.
You were wrong, my father! We travel heavy, not light.
We must take the whole heaviness, settle our feet on the earth,
Till it pushes us back, like a child through the waters of birth,

With our selves on our shoulders heavy as libraries.
All of our lives are legends, none a mere skewer of days,
But a rhythm of griefs and glimpses, a sequence of pages,
Till stiff with our binding, we fall through the last of the Stages
Glaired with the green of the world, startled by praise.

Praise for the presences here, like an open secret.
Just now outside in the wood I could almost touch it,
Elastic as bark and sure as roots, stretching and holding fast,
Certain and conscious, rejecting nothing, the past
Never a skin to slough but to wear unencumbered at last.

Neither understanding nor misunderstanding we climb
In dark, tethered to stations our shadows keep.
At night in a hole in the ground under the winds that sweep
Confusion to us all, dogged as Sherpas we climb
Up through a shuttered hole, up through cluttered sleep...

An apologia, father, for a flight to a whispering dark,
A hayfoot, strawfoot, clayfoot attempt to grow
Feathers and leaves, a wig of winds. The winds that blow
Us all, blow now to the lights of the park,
Leaves to a shuttered window. Part of the legend also.

Two

We move, tall as we like,
towards roods, through cave-runs,
grey, heraldic pillars,
broken, or not.
                    Maned horses
on the skyline
like legends
print themselves black.

Fistfuls of birds on springs,
branched candelabra, thistles,
armorial purples.
                    A stoat
shining with mouse
throats grasses, horsetails
(printed fossils in these walls)
till Jove, a brown cloudburst, warm,
of owl, twitches away the mouse.
Seconds.
Details –

make up legends:
What he said to her: irritations: 'No.
Why should I smoke your hash?
It would make me walk
through violet tassels
over the opposite hillside
crying
"Holy willow-herb!"'

God's a tail, a cirrus, whisking
behind, below, away.
I only know
the air
is whitely curled round rain.

Crouched, deaf, in a shed
(black-faced sheep, wigged judges,
stand outside, still,

but my wool has no oil),
knee-high swallows carve
fields for flies.
The way the swallows, flies, shed-roof, use it
is what I know of air.

Sulphur birds in horizons of slate
tumble precisely invisible staves of air. Careful
notes, on a dark sheet.

After so much standing
easy to think of trees
folding back like lids,
pylons moving, to scare crows.

All sleeps and fallings, meannesses,
all waiting for the heavy clock-turn, all
gladnesses,
move inside the legend like slow beasts.

Two came together, make
the legendary child
wet with messages.
Only look at him!
Dries into a man, remains
a legend.

Sermons in stones – don't hear them,
see the stones.
Empty the bag on the hill:
self, stones, inside-weather.
Stand inside
staring,
eyes circled in skull,
child in the arms
or on the arm of a child,
staring in dark at white
ounces of burning birds,
fossils, curled mist, horses,
trees
like bars.
Believing in magic,

coolly.
Until the brown cloudburst.

The world
is logical as cards.
Plays us.
We play,
legendary, blindly, deafly,
deftly. Deaf Gods.
Dear. In magic, printed in white air.

Three

The telephone drills into a pool of silence
Calling to London, Dublin, calling away
To a world thought by some to be glamorous, some superficial,
In fact to a trade like any other,
            Neither green nor grey.

A disturbance perhaps? Perhaps. With the nerve of a Blondin
We might stand on the sag of the slack-rope over Niagara
Till the crash and the spume and the yellow boiling below
Came up through the footsoles, entered the head and there was no
            Blondin anymore

But an apotheosis of spray. Perhaps. But as
For the rest of us Blondin's balancing act
Lands back on crowded banks, his diamond tights
Spangled with drying splashes. We can never stand quite
            Still, in fact

Air is not for standing. Water falls
Because it has to from a high place to a low.
As telephones remind, we are not still.
The going of water is white and noisy and it's
            A glorious way to go.

But doubts resound, rebound. Given one moment longer
Poised between bird and water, what might we see?
Basso spiders singing of constellations,
Clear formulations, bright as laundry, hung
        From mouth to tree?

Shapes, colours, cloud-movements, seem to be mouthing
Relaxed languages we can almost hear.
A man is caught between two voices, theirs
Which call to fall to join them, and his own, which makes
        A separation clear.

... Corridors of whispers like old songs.
Each man has a headful. Calls he hears in sleep.
A man remembers loves more real than he is, old errors
Haunt him like catarrhs, and promises
        He cannot keep.

He calls his friends, the dead he falls to join!
They tug him on through their magnetic field.
In hosts they dandle him, blow on him like a dandelion,
Up the M1 or to Paddington, anywhere, whisperers
        Everywhere concealed.

The ground of the past is stringing with trip-flares, gossamers.
And the living entangle him in a web of fact!
Each is as real as the other! Dizzy, he tries to name things,
Asserts his toes touch pavement, slack-rope, grass,
        That he's not abstract,

Like stars he keeps a sprained geometry; like clouds,
Busy as bats, dark and quick, or white and slow,
Depending on elsewhere pressures – smudges, cauliflowers –
Not minding it seems to be either or other, being
        Clouds is what they know.

He watches the ousel, white-bibbed like a waiter,
Like a blackbird with a piece of bread in its beak,
Flying, be true to the water, curve where the water
Curves, precisely keep the crooked line
        The waters take.

Hears trees in the wind at night each making a different sound.
Beeches that hiss like straw on fire, elms that creak, cracked
They shed soft burnables, ash like an old man groans,
Tomorrow may fall entirely. At night in dark and wind each tree
       Asserts its fact.

Of these he takes to town a pantechnicon! As Cowper
Sliced carrots for his hare with shaking hand
He keeps him upright on a rope of winds
With details, small affections carefully performed. Ceremonious
       The balance of the mind.

To hold himself, a present, to the sky,
To offer up his being in a bowl, a crumb of life,
Is good. Is best. Is dangerous. It is to stand
With cold and tender feet a rope he cannot see,
       To walk a knife

Between two darks and a hundred selves all whirring
Like ill-made gyroscopes. No wonder Cowper's hand shook.
But if his feeding Tiney 'surliest of his kind'
Kept Cowper whole, in patches, that was not
       His luck, but work.

So we work on and down. Ploughland, Oxford Street,
The journey's one and interim. Driving a furniture van
Of unsystem'd adhesions, of holds we rummage among
For selves we belong to, searching to be human. And the work
       Not soon done.

Four

    What is he looking for, crossing seas
   to sweat in bars with friends and enemies, leant back
with nothing to say much, under a poisonous pink
too-high vault enskying self and drink, what does he think,
     standing relieved in the alley saluting Jupiter,
   the black Dublin sky over his cheek
     like silk, what does he think he is looking for?

What does he find? Presumably what he's after:
  sooner or later someone warms her shoes
by crossing floors towards him, in her hand
a kind of rescue, two tickets to Dreamland.
      He brushes rouge-marks of the seat from his behind…
  Our lives could be called simple if they choose
      only old answers to old questions, round and round.

      Used tickets in his pockets, in the park at Easter
  a distant figure shields her eyes like one he knew;
the East Cheam Junior Brass Band blowing hot
'Colonel Bogey', drummer three feet high – now what
      in those two sights behind his sunglasses stings his eyes wet?
  Old emotions that obstruct his view.
      His feet, turned back to find them, fail, and sweat.

                            *

That's not the whole of it. Ask again.
If he wakes in the morning with a memory of pain
(Not of his own, of someone else's), wakes in sweat,
If he refuses to make his mind go shut
On that audible whisper, is he enjoying it?
If he pulls out prettier snaps of days,
When they were all, when it was all so long ago –
What is he doing to now – to time, and place?
What is he punishing? He would like to know.

When he has walked as far as he could up a dead-
End, with nothing, hardly anything, in his head
And nothing in his eyes but two cold shoes
And they are still not empty after years,
What, when he uses the tricks that most of us use,
That make up most of our lives – hairs
Of the sex that bit him, action, drink –
What, if he's still thinking, is he sensibly to think?
That he has a grief to bear, like yours?

Some muscular mornings that seems adequate.
But now in the park and often he can hear
Garbled talk-back from the Great Broadcaster,
Who is nowhere, in the cortex, or above the bands of Easter,

Booming something he can't fathom quite and where
On earth should he be now instead of dragging about
A twangling park with a broken radio set
Not quite receiving not-quite-messages that sting his eyes wet,
Walking, walking, till he's worn his own disgusting shoes out?

*

There must be something cool to stand on.

Children run towards an ice-cream van.
They come from nowhere, all South London
houses, nearly all, are down.
The van is playing, like a xylophone,
a half a mile of corrugated iron.

There must be something, or let's all fall in.

The heart leaps up when it beholds
Price's Candleworks in greys and golds
in thin, tin light.
Its chimney's split apart
like galvanised tin thighs.
It has to rise,
the heart. Like fish on flies
it lives on what it sees.
Tower blocks.
Tower blocks.
Groups of blacks,
sun still in their turnups,
teeth whiter than the flesh of turnips.
A wind between the towers
lifts old newspapers:
TOWER BLOCK FALLS DOWN.
RACIST...FASCIST...
                              Politics is
everything, is skin, is houses.
He finds his own. He shuts it. Pays his taxes.
Keeps a wife and child. At any rate
he lives with them. And they with him.
                              The State
by no means withers away. Perhaps he does...

85

But no.
     The wife, the he, the child are dynamos
driven by merely living, driven on
humming, dreaming, through the streets of iron,
which are no man's, every man's a room
hung inconsequential as an album.
He stands in his and has

what seems the first illumination his.

Despair is shoes of iron
not to be feared.
On, are cool; on rock
of merely living hold upright.

A childhood candle he snuffs out.
Days were sepia by the light it gave.
Outside, the day acquires a nearer look.
Surprised, he tries his feet.

Warm and white inside the shoes they move.

Five

Despair as the beginning of belief? A doctrine out of fashion
          with an activist generation,
understandably – what has their faith ever done for the poor
          but institutionalise despair?
But – it's hard to believe any more in Rational Man.
          True, we no longer have public execution,
we watch it in comfort on the television.
          True, we're the boss of a few of our germs,
the nastiest ones we bottle and multiply
          against a rainy day.
True, if we have a piece of ourselves cut away
          it happens under ether;
that more nowadays are protected from tangible harms.
          Others we've given novel ways to die.

86

True we no longer throw on the streets the broken and old,
>we leave them to half-die in half-cold.
Nevertheless – better to live in the twentieth century
>than any brutal other.
At least we've noticed we're running out of solutions,
>noticed the babies floating away
in the thrown-away ablutions, our lunatic tendency to Either/Or
>either Heart or Head,
God or Man, Chastity/Bed, even – Alive/Dead.
>Which brings us back to despair.
Despair, which can make the world die on us, make us take
>the whole bottle of pills,
or prick our arms with dreams we drown inside,
>seems, like a suicide note, the will's
pathetic attempt to punish the world, or another person.
>If one of us can decide
after pro and con (with never a spiteful one)
>to hand his ticket in,
we call him that god-like man, a genuine suicide.
>Grant him the admiration
reserved for perfect detachment, like Schopenhauer's,
>envying such composure (although we find
S. kicked his female servant down the stairs
>and having crippled her spent years
trying not to pay her compensation):
>That graceful, negative stances of the mind,
with the normal sublunary tics go hand in hand.

How, then, despair?
>There's a longer-living kind
>known to everyone over thirty-five.
When early motors begin to gag and rumble,
>and hopes like cookies crumble,
when flogging sex is flogging a hard-mouthed horse
>(pleasant enough), when being alive
is to know that tomorrow will not be better but probably worse.
>And we plead for a shot of love.

But – suppose that love is neither here nor there; like weather,
>whether we notice it
or don't, is everywhere. And we're insisting blue Aegean heat
>is weather, and everything else is not.

Perhaps a particular love becomes everything jumbled together:
            hot marsh mists, sleet,
ice-routines, mirages that curl the heart, tear-monsoons
            and, worst, small unremitting rains.
And love is something we worry too much about
            and none of us lives without
however starved we feel – because we can't. A piece of string
            in the pocket, a favourite itch,
can furnish a moment, a moment of living, rich
            with layered compost,
piled with past, and the present, million movements. There's luck
            in an open eyelid.
Outside, the world like a foreign language waits to be given back
            meaning it never lost...
Though truncheons fall like stone snow. Although for thanks
            the generosities are met by tanks
and manacles and murders are the currency
            they've been in every bloody century,
life waits to twist its many shapes, we feel it happen,
            a twitch in the gut,
joy, at an idea or an apple, shaped, misshapen
            sometimes beyond recognition,
surprising a self we thought had to do without it.
            So why should not
(though hints slip through our fingers like wet soap
            seemingly gone for good;
how, when we've never had it, can a hope
            die on us which we've never understood?)
this stiffening-up, this sense of loss, be the definition,
            be love, locked inside-out?

Some see the world as a kind of examination
            with despair as one of the questions.
Youth fills one side of the sheet with spry suggestions.
            Later, on the other,
the writing should be firmer, the words few, harder,
            until with a rattle of breath
and a click of false-teeth we hand it in to whatever
            lies on the other side of death.
Now, speaking as one who's been taught not to ask
            an impossible question
in public, like 'Why are we here?'

but privately asks it like everyone
else – the concept of test, quest, the exam idea,
        though impossible to defend,
seeming to shrink our heads to school-cap size
        in a school of pointless rule –
why does a phrase of Keats' – 'The world is a vale
        of soulmaking' – always surprise
a simple agreement? Perhaps it's as well and about time
        to stand and answer my name.
I believe there are holes in the sky. Believe the dead
        real as radio-waves outside my head.
Have dreamed a spiral to a perfect air.
        And I believe in hell.
In confirmation of deprivation. I can fail.
        Not all is well.
I believe, probably from fear (fear of Nothing
        is not a bad idea),
believe in despair, in the deprived, passionate heart,
        where snakes, and ladders, start.

Six

Experience we shared
wears through, like clothes.

You move, I know, about your own affairs.

And I have news.
Our friend is in the garden of the mad.
Brown seed-bags on the ash tree – he sees bats.
Coloured robes and Woolworth bells
and Myshkin hairs.
Disturbances
like cooking smells
climb stairs.
Policemen rot the doorbells in the night.

You in a long black 'Fifties coat
(such an old snap-shot)
are present in the hall.
Shake neither head nor finger.
Smile.
Your freedom can contain this.
I remain.
I do not know what best to do,
watched by you.

I climb.
The garden yelp
disturbs the stairs.
I hold the banister.
I cannot help.

I climb into a corner of my brain.
I serve
I swerve
the prison sentence of our counterpane.

Undrugged, the room stays dark.

Bats stay seed-bags in the junkie park.

*

Too many deaths,
too many absences,
pare down.

Downstairs they're turning-on.
Visions clatter from their gramophone.
Like chocolate
they eat the eating night,
turning it to fleshy substances.
Why should they not?

Bare trees stare outward into distances.

Upstairs
the room
is hunching shoulders
round its chill.
Understanding circles to the ceiling-light.
Then the roof slides shut.

Below, the desperate
defy the night.
They mingle breaths.

Upstairs the room examines it.

'Come down!'

The room hugs silence like a sound.

'Not yet.'
Too many absences to listen at.

Below
eye bores into eye:
'Is this me?'

Upstairs the room
pushes beyond its station and its name
between two breaths
it balances –
it calls
its deaths like birds into its branches.

Seven

Retreat upon retreat
to find a ground
for feet and mind.
Though mind sees part

of mind, like body, elsewhere.
Feet down there.
Indifferent observer
with an ice balaclava.

Mind, which has gone circular,
says: 'For once, old soldier,
I'll do the watching. You
try taking over.'

*

'Perhaps the only part of me,
after all, worth love,
is him, all clown.
He pulls my high-reach down.

After all
he is the one
who takes the pain
and just plods on

So rubber-faced the rain
takes time to reach his chin
down the folds of his endurance
out and in.'

*

White having fallen in flakes of Lux,
morning of mists, variously dun.
Albert seated in the birdless wood.
The only white remaining

is on hummocks.
He's beginning again.
The world is neither warm nor cold,
like Albert, who feels nothing.

Having given up trying.
Notices drops of thaw
honestly rolled to the bottom of where they are.
The only bright thing.

Is it dead February
or dead December?
Albert
cares not to remember.

Clocks hurt him.
Wives, Albert, wars,
poke elbows at his dream:
'Hey...what time?'

He says 'OK OK'
climbing out of head.
Does badly (rudely) outside.
Gratefully climbs back, 'Where were we...'

*

Not Pierrot. Pierrot of the moon
perhaps. Not Pantaloon,
just Albert (call him) gulping his absurd
like moon-dust, like promise.

Bores him, self-disgust.
Of all he feels, the most is dross.
He never pans it.
Drinks it all.

Memory leads him.
Did it seem?
Not, he thinks. He knows he knows not
which rich seam.

*

Today he's angry. Someone took
negligently
his last cigarette.
Reactionary Albert.

Dislikes his anger. Feels it.
In sofa-corner sits, sulks, and dumb.
Hearing heads of flowers
(tended by someone, not no one)

flinching, like snails.
While to the Liberty drum
over the world's flowerbeds
Freedom Fascists come.

*

That sofa's not his own.
Nothing is. But the past
covers it, not chintz, not tatters.
Is not seen

admittedly. 'Can you not see...?'
Not bayonets he minds,
ransacking stuffing, horse-hair.
Not loss of anything.

Nothing is quite there.
He gasps, though, airless.
It is the sureness
of the blind bayoneteer!

*

Saigon pays fourteen pounds for dead
civilians over eighteen. Seven pounds the rest.
Albert on bus top turns to the next column.
To love the world outside he does his best.

Pop-singer's Twenty-first in Chamber of Horrors.
Her cake a cast in icing of her feet.
Two eyes turned frankly on it could invest
even this world with beauties he's not quite forgotten.

His own, like King's Road buses, cannot move
past a new boutique called 'God is Love'.
'Christ!' He kneels before his memories, 'Forgive
a man who has been blessed who can't bless this.'

*

A glass of wine, a glass, another glass.
Outside, the London afternoon is brass.
He holes out in a bookshop, sees the walls
Are hung with photographs of naked girls

94

with naked men, and girls with girls
also. Some girls alone
have breasts with ropes on, pulled, cruelly, at.
Their faces, close-up, act, or are in, pain.

He kneels, a knight of Eros, in the shrine.
Perhaps that pain is softness, inside out?
'Can I help you sir?' He sighs, Alas.
Inside his flesh he would live always but.

*

It floats away, even the truest book
of lovers true/untrue, of crimes and couplings
and all that, once, he cared intently for.
Too known, that tunnel, further to explore.

He stares at green on unmoved stones in water,
and rooted red also, close-to, symmetrical,
the outside wall of Brixton Methodist Chapel.
The splendid ball also that swings to smash it.

The innocence of Things (an old religion).
Other times, other innocencies. Underground
constructed pages flap back down the tunnel:
tube-train faces, washed in air, like pebbles, are his own.

*

Glimmerings and decays.
Now Albert only sees himself
in D.H. Evans' window.
His face a time-scape in a camera obscura

that includes the future
(at the edge therefore
himself no longer there).
Not good – feels something move

– finds a Gents in Holborn
with plumbing like a monsoon
and a macintoshed city love-guardian
eternally peeing policeman.

95

He doesn't know what yellow stars the path.
Pain has names sometimes – joy has too.
Which comes. He stops and shoves his nose
inside a pink-white hedge, white elder, pink dogrose.

The air inside – a sauna bath!
Colour, smell, nothing can change; not news,
not dead greenfinch sticking to the tar.
'Pain and joy are only inside-weather.

'Like Hardy, leant upon a coppice gate,
I'll take and break an old thermometer.
Not hot nor chill can I avoid or choose.
One comes sometimes, sometimes' he shakes the gate 'the other goes

*

(Days pile on.)
Addresses infant son.
'Three times a day you're fed a meal.
Three years

before you remember one.
Your life's a dream of growing.
'Cheers' he lifts his cup
'so's mine.

'You know – I like you. Our every ill
comes not so much from never sitting still
as from dreaming we are woken up.'
His son observes the words, like noises snowing.

*

He breathes – the air!
'My dears – I wish you well. I wish
you well – but stand away from me,
an empty dish. And no,

not cruel. See the sky
fill the empty tree.
I am full.
I am what I have. No more. No

more. The sky is wine –
it washes. Oh – the air –
I am a back
I follow through a door.'

Eight

Car, arrived in shed, disturbs the wren.
A life of movement. And a life of silence.
Wren gone, the car cools, ticks. The shed drips.

As to an aeroplane a tunnel clips
Darkness aware of green. Trees lead down
Aisles of birds asleep in rows.

Under a ceiling scratched and earthed by boughs –
Circuits of silence. A tuning-in
To batteries of birds. Some valves unclose.

Radar of the night now pings with echoes.
Now is the time for winging-in of ghosts.
Two feet in muddy suede. A dying fire.

> These soles have stood in galleries and bars,
> In trains and in urinals (where a man
> Walked on his heels, a penguin, keeping clean).

> He thinks: a dying bed goes still, the scene
> (Not a second and the trolley clangs)
> An aviary of sympathetic aprons.

> Blurring the outline of the pointed stone,
> Silence, these ghosts fly in to feed on,
> Furling warm wings round...

Breath poises in the ribcage. Silence swells: a sound
Of vaulted halls flurried above with birds
In and out a high bright window.

Cups and the table, feet, below in shadow,
Fall like feathers to their inward weight.
Coloured ghosts, sparks, stir up the air.

The room's unstartled by a glowing chair.
Attention settles like a flock of birds, shapes,
The way a scarf shapes thrown upon a bed.

'Come in, ghosts! if this silence is your bread!'
Life is so prodigal. Devoted now to white
Swan silences it still wholly lives...

The window catches sparrows bright as olives,
Luminous against an obscure dawn;
Winter grass with yellow in its beak

Suspended, powdering, mote-like
Towards the arched swords, shining, of the dead,
The friendly marriage-swords, the lonely things

Of God. (Mere grasses, starling
Picked-between, and boiling wren.) Wet pigeons' wings
Beat deeply, frightened, in the moist white air...

Cold. A dying fire.
Returning random weightlessness again.
Grey seagulls quarrelling in tractor-light

Morning. Eyes gone skin-tight.
Drinking. Nude dreams over the cider-butt.
Engines pumping. Rolling. On and on.

White face in the cockpit. Contact gone.
'Can't stop moving. Engine. Cannot hear you.'
Crash on silence. Useless stubs of penguin wings.

Latent light in circles round fence-posts, in rings
Of algae patience. Our light. Distant silences
Still sonorous with new arrivings.

Nine

The fire is out. The fire has to be relaid.
So, up the bank in the wind. Dipper curves the lake,
cries a radar bleep like an audible bat.
             Against dark
its plumage vanishes, the white blob on its throat,
alone, floats faster than a ping-pong ball.
It stops on a half-sunk bough, dips, lives anxiously locked
             behind the waterfall.
The wood's crosshatched with fallen timber. Smells
of deaths, bird-droppings, mice, white spongy weed-roots.
Sweats, cracks; then – still as a graveyard.
             Some timber, fallen, rots,
turns to water, you tell by the sound and feel
of a boot-kick, smell. Earth sucks it back.
Other goes heavy, hard, weighs into itself.
             Sodden, black,
mud-encrusted, smelling of earthworms, beech is best.
Sawn, is neat, compacted, white inside,
burns slowly, making whitest ash.
             The wood...
To enter the wood is like walking into a bottle.
Thin low weeds throw globe shadows of green,
balloons of green balancing greys and brown.
             In between,
thinly, are paths of precise deer.
A tunneller heaves on its back a line of sog.
Tree-creepers pick at crevices, vertical mice.
             A perfect log –
beech – a liftable length. Pivot on thinner end
cracking through kindling, stamping dogmercury juice
shoulder in balancing place and – up.
             A sluice
down slithering mudbanks, collar collecting woodlice,
slaloming conifers, not to wedge the tail.
Fifteen feet long, nine inches across, rested at last
             on the bank-rail.
Gasping, knees bent like a coolie's, clapped
by two-year old from the cottage (he can't understand
why his applause is soundless, ball of thumb

on heel of hand,
elbows too close to side)...Describe. Describe
this ringing, glass-rim noise, a tongueless bell
we seem inside, while moments hit the side of it like rain
and real rains fall...
Things stand around like sentinels, like bells with flame-tongues –
there's flame inside the curry-coloured hare –
swinging in green between trees creaking, falling.
Guarding where?
These oddly burning things do not seem traps. Human skins
measure the wind, human watering eyes and listenings –
while thin suns circle trees. We may
be saved by things.
Ears swivel like deer's, like radar-saucers.
What do we, listening (should we listen) hear?
Where? What fire? What is this talking about?
Real shadow-theatre!
Space hangs burning, moments drown in it, Furies dragging
memories through ice; then, in ice, a grey
armpit stain of thaw: warm, underground waters. Glimmerings
and decay.
We are separate. We spiral up, like grasses, never join.
Each point of a blade, it seems, is meant to take
soundings of air, fire-eater, that it breathes;
and not mistake
deaf ears for no sound. Sociable as a hayfield!
Or ships in ice, by lamp keeping station,
(signals through dark, jokes, formal as kisses through a grid),
convoys of separation!
Faces pouched with freight of an unseen
that lives in the hold whether we wish or no.
Perhaps a white arrival? Triumphant shouts made echoless
by endless snow.
On. That coast is no coast. Ice. Love
is the hug of a thermos'd anorak, it shows
as destinations, sweeps of furtherness. A brotherhood
of ice-floes!

'Domesticities – the finest earth can show'
(said Cowper) never, nobly, quite enough – fine though.
A touch of seedless air burns through those furs.
But make the fire.

100

Under the tongueless bell the place stares.
To show one's love before it slips away!
To catch at a place and hold this
                    scraping tree,
this dark, this damp smell on the dark stair,
this half-moon window, bag for a whole wind: a caul
shadowed with lamps, and hands, a child's shoe...
                    Outside the wall
a wind that can kill a man, fling trees down,
makes fire smoke, makes eyes sting that stare
for fire hanging, tongues, in bells of air.

Ten

Fleeing from colleagues to The Versailles
                    Restaurant, Queen's Hotel, Leeds,
alone in a corner in splendour, it's difficult
                    after four glasses of solitary wine
to keep one's lips still when one's talking
                    to the other, empty, chair.
This room is a dream of a shared palace;
                    even three shallow steps
for entrancing down; warmly breathing money
                    drifts up an arras,
behind it a Polish waiter draws on a butt
                    and rests his face.
Outside, sharp, blind buildings
                    slice wind into streets,
people like sticks angle their faces away
                    from sodium lighting,
whittled by winds and horrible architecture.

                    You'll be a matchstick too,
blown down flues of cities, striding adjacent moors
                    in John Buchan rain,
still a dry mannikin, making macintoshed gestures,
                    the future crammed with you.
Tonight I'll call you eighteen, adding sixteen

years, me fifty-three,
your dad pop pater father
        with broken veins in his nose
etcetera. 'I've called you here'
        (I cannot believe
this wine is mine and so I drink it, addressing
        an empty chair
in an absurd corner of an unknown city)
        'to thank you.'
Your not being here but asleep
        in a dripping wood
with vats of mothers' honey still to tap
        makes it easier
to thank you. 'Thank you.
        Merely by being
you showed me valves of the heart
        still pumped, like gills.
And may the same happen to you whatever
        the reason.'
                You've laced
your fingers between your knees, your head
        bends over your plate
with an awkward adolescent hairfall.
        I'll never say this.
Or insist how little of me, your age, has changed
        except for outwards;
how invisibly little the drip affects the limestone
        cave-runs we look out from.
Of course not. In sixteen years I'll spare you that;
        a buff, embarrassed, with his son.
A shame in some ways. 'I loved you so much – how
        you astonished me!
you made me – you made me think again.'
        Dreadful! How could you endure it?
Begin again:
                'I ought,
Being so much older, and your father,
        to say something
about life and how to live it. Well –
        It's a series of beginnings.
Beginnings again, from beginnings, like a river.
        That's it! A mortal

Again and Again!'
                    Ash is scattered
          over the clover-shaped
butter-pats – I smudge them trying to clean them:
          the nearest foursome
is angled as though in a wind, trying to listen.
          'Listen. You
were a new beginning. So
          you owe me nothing!'

Soils, shafts, ancient geologies dictate
          the unstraight course of a river.
I shall never know anything of your turnings.
          You were one of mine.

Small rocks, uprooted flowers, dead birds,
          we carry with us, grit,
detergent, dying fish. Too big
          a blockage and unashamed
we shoulder back (we should), right-angle, shrink,
          expand; find ways round. Stopped
once and for all, we dreadfully explode. Niagara.
          Underneath us float
rooted, wafting greens, Ophelia's hair.

          You sprained my flow
into a fresher landscape. Or rather, same old greens,
          different water.

Starvations, tortures, manacles
          are facts we
force a way through (and do not speak of here, art
          can't deal with it,
can't breath Cyklon B – don't try. Art exists
          face to face with its
antithesis; defies, defines its opposite)
          These facts are forms
of fear. Are doomed attempts to stick
          too long
behind the shelter-rock of one idea.
          It brings such dooms in wake –
the flow refused – such burstings out!

You know –
I would not dredge a stream,
        would not murder weeds
more sure of place than we are, would not move
        until I had permission from the air.
The world's a language that we think
        we only speak
when we decline it harshly. Everything is breathing.
        We only think
we think we do not hear.
        This room, like water's breathing.
The cold stones of the city, hear them hawk!
        We are passengers
of our own misting breaths. We two, the same!
        Although I am your father,
you, my son...
                'Have I been silent long'
        My boiled eyes
scour the room.

        Sex? I've thought
of not much else for years, and that's
        my history, not yours...
Let it take you down the estuaries of silt
        until you see
perspectives of horizons poised like birds.
        Listen
to the weir below your ribs.
        Listen to the fear
in dirty jokes. Hear the laughter
        also. Oh my dear
how can I know if you'll have the hands of a juggler,
        able to keep
light and dark in the air at once and not
        go boss-eyed! How can I know
you'll have the heart!
                        You're not
        listening and I
have not spoken. Your father
        and his father
do not, did not, know.

'Do not believe
anything anyone tells you.'
I have you now of course. You lift your head
and grin – and hearts
can nearly burst with unimpartable information:
That we're the same,
brothers, twins, your species, you're not new! –

Keep calm. There's a journey to be gone
by focussing on the table-cloth: there's flax
there's yellow straw
below wet stars, there's sleep, where opposites
collide, sometimes become
old, slept-in, laundered linen bed-sheets
soft on limbs as water.
Though when we wake we've grown nothing but whiskers,
where were we then?
How dared we dream of carelessness when selves
shrink to pin men
on a railway platform left behind,
the world
fronding out towards us like a fan,
movement and counter-movement,
gathering tighter, clearer?
'Waiter!

Well –
I won't keep you. Be off to your party.'
I want you
to be wholly alive, which is to say
to be good. 'Be good.'

Is there a party? Perhaps you only invent one,
wanting to hug a self-hood,
a mystery, feeling it form
a calyx round your bud.
Will you one day be able to give it
to someone? Will there be one
or merely be too many?
Will the world one day
for you, as at times it astonished your father
(you helped him)

be open-mouthed, and breathe?
        Will you hear it?
Or will your bud
        nipped by yourself, or broken
by such easy mistimings, fate, or character,
        whirl in a pool of cold,
blackened, embittering the water?
        We all need
such luck...
                I catch your shifty grin.
                'Good night.' You turn your head.

I watch you watch your father
        go half-drunk to bed.

EDWARD THOMAS IN HEAVEN

(1974)

Occasional Birds

Morning white as a sheet of paper
I watch you with trepidation, still propped on my pillow,
Begin with a mist emitting occasional birds.
By moving so precisely (outside the world looks blind)
They seem to suggest there is some place
To go to when they leave the mist behind.

Pulling on socks I wonder
What are the chances today of being included
Just for a moment inside that talkative silence:
Feeling time, like a mammoth, steaming and black,
Slurp up through the swamp not knowing there's a howdah
Of confident birds like jewels on his back

– Time moving and the bright birds still.
But morning fills the head with too much noise.
Moth-memories come banging to get in.
So, cram a casque over an empty skull
And face the mist, a morning like a wall.
An absent man gone walking in a pearl.

Verisimilitude: I take a child
Walking towards the slow-appearing trees.
His chatter sounds appropriate and wise,
Granting small features to a world born flat.
We walk inside the birthday of the world.
I wear his newness like a birthday hat.

Discern small things with him. Begin
With smallness, stillness, as the skin of pearl
Thins round us and the sun pricks in.
Our tree becomes a wood. I see him ride,
Quite still, the back of time, I see him go...
I love an absence sitting by my side.

I love the trees revealed, the way
Light rinses fog from colours, opens out.
I love a size that does not care for me.
I have a skull so empty that I float.
I love the vertigo! I love the cold!...
Cold. I bend to button up his coat.

Sometimes

There was one who was perfect, who had
faults doubtless, but they were for God
to see, not for us who loved her, though whatever
I think of her is usually mixed with my
own falling short. But sometimes I see her
as she was, nothing to do with me:

as sometimes a cloud leaves the sun alone
and every leaf on a tree is a plate for light,
the tree become solely itself, and stays itself
though another cloud crosses and it goes dull again,
its secret kept; puzzled at by the eyes
of one who wants it always to stay gilded,
isolated, amazing: resentful of its patience,
obscuringly angered he only sometimes sees.

For Bruno

Baby, you fight the air, your feet splash it.
You push with wrists at something there.
Your father likewise gropes in air for contact,
Bumped by crowds of dead souls on the stair,
Buffeting his body, strings of shocks.

He walks outside and eats the mist,
Invites the winds and leaves inside his coat.
He stands in bogs and snuffs up bog-breath, small
Moats of silence round each boot.
He cups his ear to stone-talk.
Birds bubble through mist, grass grows horses.
Night's the same house, a ghosts' walk.

You bubble in his shadow and you'll think it
Odd he's on a journey through the house
And hasn't left his shadow for your blanket.
But when we're called away we have to go,
And shadows never warm. He watches you
Paddle wrists through fireflies round your rug,
Angels with meteor tails – and demons, yes.
And uncoaxed dead. Though you may grow to find him
Tapping barometers with his cheeks sunk in,
Or caught in the apple tree, algae in his hair,
Bubbling greenly – still, he'd have you walk
As tenderly, baby, through the loaded air.

October

Perched on a branch October
Puffs out dark.
Below the barn a farmer
Shoots his small bore,
Makes the sound of a book
Thrown flat on the floor.
Round their transistor
Straw balers take shelter
In Radio One and straw.
Blackbirds immune to boredom
Go on, go on
Clicking in hawthorn.
Orange beaks glow.

Out on a limb I remember
Nothing clear.
A wisp of cloud
I am my own
Unfeatured atmosphere.
Seem a kind of tree-smoke,
All ways blown.
I love my children,
When I look

They're going, gone.
The mist I am
Must feel a sham
Place for you to perch on.

The warm stuff of memory
Is nonsense really.
Cold meat.
Something you taught me –
I forget.
Mist in the branches
Shrinks and is gone.
Birds sometimes use me
To make scatters from.
You didn't choose me,
Not as I am.
Why don't you lose me?
Perhaps you have done.

Commuter

Deaf and dumb lovers in a misty dawn
On an open station platform in the Dordogne
Watched each other's hands and faces,
Making shapes with their fingers, tapping their palms
Then stopped and smiled and threw themselves
Open-mouthed into each other's arms

While the rest of us waited, standing beside our cases.
When it arrived she left him and climbed on the train
Her face like dawn because of their conversation.
She suddenly turned, grabbed his neck in the crook of her arm,
Gave him the bones of her head, the bones of her body, violently,
Then climbed on again alone. Her face hardened
In seconds as the train moved away from her island.
Tight lipped she looked around for a seat on the sea.

The Day of the Shoot

Some beaters in the mist go 'Purrl...Whirrl...'
Coaxing pheasants to rise, others bash and snarl
As though they hated the birds, as they would bully cattle.
Three burnished round-eyed cocks try not to startle,
Run stiff-legged, heads down, along the road
Hidden from guns. Smaller birds are pellets, hurtle, scared.

At the top of the hill, from the hole of the old quarry
Sticks a crystalled vacuum cleaner and part of a Morris chassis.

No sound, except a shot, or the shout of a beater,
Now distant, and the continuous traffic murmur that is everywhere.
Out of the white a figure like a pear drifts up,
With a beater's stick, an old dog, and a short pipe.
Moving as slowly as the mist moves, skiving his beater's fee,
Old Bill Messenger narrows eyes at the white day.
It nibbles his overcoats, narrows his figure,
He drifts slowly off, a piece of weather.

Rattling hogweed has petals of frozen air;
Furry grasstufts are shoulder muscles of a polar bear.

Whiter shafts, on white, scaffold a wigwam sky
A burst of starlings pushes at and is pushed down by,
Just at the day's low edge, a sag of bird.
A blur of gold, a grail, is soaking downward
Over the squatter's barn, the iron roof is shining black
That Tom soon must quit – Mist rolls back.

White grass already melted green.
Mottled walls, purple shadows on smooth hills soaked clean.
The bull in breath-fog lifts its head to stare
Again at time and place. You brought me here.

Looking down at shining grass making my ankles wet,
Surprised, I remember you would have been thirty eight
In a month. Clean-cut boles of yellow trees, prinked grass,
Behind clear fields horizons made of glass
Make a bowl no wider than the mist. Thinking 'Thirty eight...'

Brushing russet pheasant droppings from a gate,
I climb to get back home. Such confident bangs climb up
To where a man dissolved, with dog, and pipe.

Eclogue

A:　Where pigeons waddle as though they've wet themselves,
　　Deaf to the traffic, alert only to competition,
　　Flying only to roost, or jump the queue,
　　I take my pleasure among man-made fountains,
　　With Landseer's ridiculous lions, and I jump too,
　　　　A man among others in the imperfect city.

B:　Down combes in boots I put up flocks of fieldfares,
　　Brown and slate pecking at thin snow.
　　They fly like divers, wings to side, and click.
　　Settled in trees, from underneath they're white
　　As sky, the colours of earth each back.
　　　　And everywhere I stand, the sound of water.

A:　Among my telephones I think of you.
　　I rub against the clutter of the world
　　While you count catkins in your shrinking patch.
　　Where are the other people in your landscape?
　　Where do you put whatever it is you catch
　　　　Of reasons twinking from the tails of wrens,
　　My nature-philatelist? Who do you give them to,
　　My mud-gourmet?
　　　　　　　　　　　Standing with you today
　　In a scoop between three fields, leant on a gate,
　　I see it's beautiful, I see the evening light.
　　I also see the world's a mad machine – Who puts it right
　　Hiding in valleys of privileged pastoral?

B:　And I see green stuck on your thumb and finger
　　From the gate. Lichen, algae, crumble the gate back
　　Into earth. Their living shines. Some evenings

When the light is right this gate can glow
So green it sends out ripples through the air, rings,
   Loops, lassos of living light.

A: So you go sprouting lichen of your own?
     Thus the more or less permanent five-day's growth?
     And where in God's name did you get that hat?
     Go Rustic (where's your tractor? cow-shed? gun?)
     But as a spectator aren't you over-doing it?
       Your greatest challenge is which way to walk.

B: It's true your talk can sometimes make me itch
     With –

A: Hatred of me?

B: a wish to scratch myself.
     There's not a thing you say that birds don't shout.
     Empty bellies can't see Views. Agreed.
     And, oh, agreed. And yet – 'The happy man is right.'

A: His happiness is built on others' backs.

B: But you are happy?

A: No by God I'm not!
     What's happiness when we've so far to go
     Before pinched lives unfold in your fine shades,
     Sprawling with Saturday gestures on their earth,
     And when they do it's bye-bye solitudes,
       Bye-bye philately, your fields are full!

B: I'd wish to be a man among such men.
     And there's no answer to the argument except
     I didn't choose a role, the role chose me.
     Perhaps there should be one man in a field
     Standing absurd in a duffle coat watching a tree.
       Because it's always moving, always still.

A: You mean – 'Why shouldn't I gobble the menu?
     The beggars are kept in a different postal district.'
     You call impotence insight while the knives
     Of starving children's bones break through their skin.

B: I peer inside the tunnels of our lives
     And make some peace with maggot and with mole.
   I sense a honeycomb of dark and light
   We have to eat before we slip away
   (And I mean die). I cannot love your luke-warm house
   Half-way. Kindness, justice, these are duties, but
   Stick to mouse-traps and you catch a mouse.
     I'd wish my friends a wilder fate than that.

A: You've friends, of course, in the rice-queue? What you love
   Is death. You want to snuggle into it and snooze.
   Well go ahead then, die.

B: Dead men can't watch a tree.
   We fear each other and we both know why:
   I can be you but you can not be me . . .

A: Man is my concern, and mind of man –

B: You know I hardly care for man at all.
   I care for you of course – we can't be parted.
   Like you, and Swift, I care for Tom and Dick and Harry . . .
   But let's go in – this thorn tree's turning black.

A: My friend, I quit without regret reactionary
     Dreams of dignity among doomed sheep.

B: My friend, I leave regretfully a sight
   Of ash-tree tops holding the last of the sun.
   Our glimpses gone, they never come again.
   These trees don't know how insecure they are.
   Behind their backs the saw-scream has begun.
     They hold the sun because they hold their height.

A: And you can't be as ignorant as that.
   You fear the death that creeps behind your back.
   You suck for comfort on their rootedness
   But you can't live on minerals and air,
   Your roots are feeding elsewhere, among men,
     Your food is in the world you run away from.

B: What makes you think the trees don't frighten me?
For once, just once, just look . . . At times I'm scared to death!

A: See? Death again . . .

B: Or scared back into life.
Look – we're back at the house.
Switch on the light.
I'll just go up and settle my
Sons down for the night.

A: '*My*' sons, never 'children',
Always '*mine*'.

B: That's right.
Uncork my wine.
I'll be as quick as I can.

A: Be as long as you like,
You can't escape, we're stuck,
Pigs in a poke.
But, after so much watching,
When do we have your report?

B: Not before your bulldozers
Cut the watching short.

A: You mean, you lose?

B: I mean, you cannot choose.

Game

The sky is blue and still.
Standing on winter corn
The shooters on the hill
Are black on green.
Each an expensive man,
His gun stiff and keen.
Fat with hand-fed grain
A pheasant trapped in thorn
Flaps to rise and bang
Doesn't try again.

The Famous Poet

Even has it in for skylarks.
Scowls up and writes his dark scowl down.
His greatest passion – *Not to be deceived*.
He writes this, and the world sighs 'Strong!'

Even the Man in the Moon has a torn face...
He hulks behind his door, his dark
Scuttles with ghost-crabs – he knows Life!
And snarls first, right in the teeth of Life's snarl.

His almost friend, elbow on the grass,
Forgives the skylark Shelley, sees a bird
Striated brown, notably nervous,
Scattering notes, confetti, from its note-bag.

Observes, later, the moon is neither torn
Nor caring, is the moon. Certainly the hours
Of grass were not, could not be, wholly unhappy.
It smelled well, the lark for company.

Ants and horseflies, just, under control.
He wades through the grass down the hill and knocks on the door.
The other is standing inspecting his walls for blood.
Sighing – he'd hoped for a drink other than rats' sperm –

Outside he is forced in the cowparsley. Two charabancs
Of Poetry Students in summery clothes necking and laughing.
In dove-light he watches them straighten their clothes and faces,
Thrilled, soon, to frown in the presence of Truth.

Sentimental Education

He finds he wraps up warm to think of her.
Warmth with her is what he best remembers.
Sitting indoors in overcoat and mufflers
He lets the room go dark.
Finding it helps, an odorous warmth, to remember hers.

Dressed like a man who expects to be called away,
In a coat he doesn't belong to the room quite.
He slumps in a chair by the clock and the fire, temporary,
Was it in the angle of her head?
Her head stays fair, his head is thin and white.

Why could she not have stayed, grown old?
What was it he saw in his dream that made him laugh out loud?
She was a murderess, she had cut up
Three bodies neatly.
Why three? Because he alone knew her secret he was proud.

She had put the bodies together again like jigsaws.
On their chests were red lines thin as hairs.
Did she do that to him, cut him in pieces
By going? An old Orpheus
Was he, held together by overcoats and chairs?

How he'd enjoyed that dream! A murderess...
He no longer had to live up to her, like a Muse,
They were fellow conspirators – in the dream that was.
Awake he is always clogged
Alone, like a stick in a weir, and no dream-flood rescues.

He aches in all his parts. He does not see in his child
A greed for his life; he shields a fading joy, a naked spirit.
In his own room he huddles in front of the fire.
But if it's the child at his door,
Without his overcoat he opens it.

He doesn't need holding together in front of the child.
What shall I do – what DO we do with the dead?
He does not mind his pieces loose between them.
Wherein did it lie?
In her eyes? Her feet? In things she said?

When I leave this life will I find out?
But she was, even more than the other things, was this life.
In dreams she turns away, laughing, she ignores me.
Looks lovingly only,
And I love her most, a goddess, cutting lives up with a knife.

Lover of Quietness

'Life has slowed to a crawl-pace. That's too fast.
Under my hair bees hive and ignore me.
Waiting, stroking tree bark like God's-skin
I itch among grasses for honey to be ready.

There are such tall stretched silences
I will not be buzzed out of.
I am my own bee, though.
I stretch towards low clouds while children eat my ankles.

I topple nowhere, I am ridiculous.
A giraffe neck and ridiculous raw ankles.
God laughs unkindly but I cannot mind,
Busy with moisture flying past my tongue.

God sucks my honey and he leaves me empty.
His empty vessel which he will not fill.
White moisture my head is among wears me away.
At times – I have a consciousness of bone

Of picked cleanness that curves through stars through spaces,
Stands with other white presences none of them noticing,
In the huge warmth of an ideal indifference:
Unitchy self-hoods. And me a beautiful thing – like everything.'

Consolations

Sir, these are very boring angels I talk to,
Not much bigger than bees, not wiser than owls,
Very rapidly nodding little bee-heads
'More Sir, please.'

I do the talking, I'm so excited. They don't talk.
At first – What a relief to know they existed
And hear them agree with me! Though I perhaps invented
Their gasps and sighs.

Yes I know I should clean and refrigerate my barn,
Be cold and alone with a table and a question.
But I'm scared to be cold and I've come to rely on
Their little wings for breeze.

Besides, outside there's a big one, his back against a tree.
His folded wings, the lines of his leaning body
Are greenest in evening light. Yawning, he watches my angels
Like somebody else's fleas.

And under indifferent lids he watches me.
He stays out there. The conversations with small ones
Are a try-on of course, a work-out, a search for a phrase
To make him rise,

Settle his pinions exactly, and calm as a camel
Enter to a pleased disappearance of small ones.
These days are a sweated rehearsal for talk with an angel
Full Size

Who is certainly out there, feeling the downdraft of pigeons,
Smelling the rain on nettles, watching small raindrops
Make leaves jump, as though a bird in the nettle-clump
Hopped for flies.

Brushing pollen and barleyseed from his aërial robes
He'll sit looking past me pretending to look at nothing
Abstractedly keeping a deep angelic boredom
Almost out of his eyes.

'I always knew you were there, that you would come!'
His pupils are tiny from watching huge distances.
He stands up exasperated, his rainbow wings unfurled
By talkative surprise.

Leaves me behind with an undinted easychair and an idea
Of a cool with no shudder, a cold that warms me through,
But no proof at all, not a feather, not even a
Consolation Prize.

Real Sky

I lean back like a baby on this wind.
Though walking I lean back, as though
On a spinnaker, on the wind's round hand.
A moment comes, and I'm a bony cloud,
A part of being, and my coat's my shroud.

I wear my grave-clothes and I do not mind.
Small trills escape from small birds suddenly:
I'm going nowhere and the thought's my friend.
All things are stirring upwards into air,
Not fighting time, for time is what we are.

That's how the dead retain their dignity.
They have not fallen, are not felled at all.
Exist, exist in time as much as we.
Why take such comfort from small signs of Spring?
This frozen wind is quite as real a thing.

I walk through deathbeds as I'd walk a moor
That's been plumped and freshened by the snow.
No saw-teeth, screaming, make a tree unsure.
Around me, stones are confident as words.
Cold slowly closes eyelids of dead birds

That should look humbled, flattened – they do not.
Weeks afterwards, the debris of the hare
Still lives inside the echo of the shot.
Eternity loves time, I hear it blow
Between doomed grasses and I see them glow.

I never was on speaking terms with Gods.
Baby-like I lie on what I see.
Babies, gifted with such empty heads
Are briefly unsurprised by talking stones,
Unfrightened briefly by the hare's white bones

And I remember briefly how they feel,
My bones supported by the wind's round hand.
A life-long love affair – I wooed the real;
At last I see the real world expand,
And real sky come plucking for my hand.

Winterpraise

In lands of perpetual summer
Cranes fly slowly. Death is around.
Huge leaves. Green is dangerous.

Laughing soldiers in jeeps, usually.
One foot on the dashboard.
Worn by loose pistols.

A seamless boredom, a sky soldered.
Any time the time for planting rice,
Eating rice, standing, squatting,
Green leafplate, three fingerfuls.
Jokes are eyecrinkle, teeth.
The rest, obsidian staring.

Cranes, high, their wings miming a funeral
There was no time for.
River, ants, were quicker.

*

In lands of cold lanes
Dead birds are broken stoves
That burned roundly.
Hurtled, not that slow wing-flap.
Even the slow
Buzzard hangs on a wire of attention.

In overgrown orchards
Seeds balance on grasses, then
Puffs of seedsmoke.

Winds like yardbrooms.

In seasons of humorous overcoats,
Death, not a fly at the nostril,
A slow hardening

– Could be seen so.

An iron day.
Another place.

November the First

A long farewell.
An All Souls' Day so bright I shift my seat
Out of the glare and dead flies blacken the sill.

One window crawls.
The other taps with blown birds' beaks, torn leaves.
Today's a windy tunnel of farewells.

Farewell red-coated figure
Playing trains down lanes hairy with November.
We'll play the same again, next year, sometime, never.

A silly game,
My longing is, to keep you, when the sun
Never lights one blade of grass the same

Minute by minute.
Farewell's the only word wind ever says
And all we say is soundlessly lost in it.

Time blows
Clearest and clean round those who do not dream
Heavenly Waiting Rooms of renewed Hallos.

Farewell red back.
I shall always dream so, mustily. Goodbye
Till then, red engine, on your single track.

A Box of Sons

A box of sons on wheels;
A father with no sense
Of anything his own,
Himself or either son;
Are margined by the frills
And feathers of a June.

Like worlds the pramwheels roll
Imaginary edges.
Soon all three will go
Cartwheeling through the slow
Motion of the soul
Dumb as snow.

He thinks he hates the thought.
All changes fur the heart.
Heart, furred or not
Believes in broad daylight
It sees the globes, white,
Of souls that fall through night.

Like the Heron

By poison maddened, the heron
Begins to eat his children.
Not only fish, his own
Eggs he stabs his beak
In – his nest floods with yolk.

Not quite flowering, sprayed
Cowparsley at the roadside
Bends to bury its head –
The nape below the bud
Is delicate pink, the quick
Flesh of a fingernail –
For a slaughtered mile.

Last summer in a pushchair
A child who now can walk
Was brushed by plates of white
Blossoming, bird-rocked. In winter
When the stalks had dried
He used them as a sword.
Now eagerly he walks
Past pink collapsed necks.

Spring itself, the boy
Pulls, I pull away
From more lives flattened.
Could almost beat the boy.
Like the heron poisoned.

All I Want

All I want to do is sleep
(Anything to stop me smoking!)
And listen to the wind above the roof.
Ashes and fires remind me of the dead.
Something has been murdered in my head.
Lucky hugs and kisses helped me then,
Now I only hear the choking
Voices of the children.
The banked horrors have been a-stoking.
I tried hard. Underneath
They burnt me hollow in my sleep.
In chairs I close my eyes, my grinding teeth
Make me jump up.
Before, I was a sprauncy pup.
I told you joking
Would see us through.
I lied to you.
I see it now, with my wonky eye.
One man's crumble,
I know it, does not edify.
Is only true.
I do not like myself at all.
Only a short way to fall.
I wanted to make a thing for you to keep.
I cannot do it.
A hole rots through it.
I wanted to make a thing for you to keep.
All I want to do is sleep.

Child's Walk

Climbing a rabbity bank his breath smokes
Among thistles hung with spiders' webs like hammocks,
White with dew still, in the wood's dark shadow.
In a tangle of brambles, ash trees, mossy elders,
He picks cold blackberries sat on his father's shoulders.
The whole soggy wood to the top is an old rubbish tip
Of a cottage that's gone. Under a log
Finds an Ovaltine lid, knows it is Ovaltine
Because of the Ovaltine writing. Lies by a bog,
In the open, caught in a serial story he is inventing.
Stands on a rock in the stream to pee in the wind,
Watching it drift. Holding a broken
Kettle abstractedly holds out the other hand
As a gift, to be taken.
                              As light slowly goes
Asks a quiet question about a pigeon
Lying below him upside down with curled toes.

Spencer Park

An engine of infinite delicacy
Is helping an older girl
Throw a ball for a shiny black dog called Tara.
'Tara, because he is shiny and black like tar?'
A father
Is watching and wishing
The smile held forever.
Ball and girl and dog
The same forever.
Cannot prevent the impossible prayer:
An arch
Over the bright machine
Only a perfect lover
Can ever enter.
He sits on a bench in the park

And badly his heart spins.
Mad he is not he is
Right he is not
Thinking about himself is
Watching an engine of infinite delicacy.

Driving Back

A pale face, a hand relinquished at the schoolroom door.
'I cannot stay to explain everything any more.'
Driving back the hills are dark, a storm holds off.
Later, in the pub, he says 'I'm scared. A boy begins his life.
I fear the relinquished hand, the slow hardening,
Fear his vanities, lusts, losses – fear *everything*!
His life-long search for somebody's hand to hold,
His freshness of heart growing stale, then cold.'

'But mightn't he find a hand his flesh to cherish?
Never learn your vanities and his heart stay fresh?'
'Life's a flooding tunnel where we drown.
I've just watched a trusting back go in.
Think of your minds, the way they think, and can you hope?'
All of his selves looked down at the floor and none spoke.

Opened and Fastened

Opened and fastened, the empty satchel, so often,
The fabric is torn and the luminous plastic broken.
Small children are learning to be important.
One of them notices raindrops hitting the lane
Splash up, rimmed with knobs like a little crown.
He tells his teacher this; she says Sit down.

Unable to bear the thought of this taming I want
To lie on the hill in the rain and drown
Every instilled importance. Be flattened down
As the grass on the hill is bent white by the rain
That bounces the lane of the airy terrapin
Building the puzzled children fasten, unfasten empty satchels in.

Picture a Father

Picture a father running up a lane
Sweating into his old clothes. Training.
Three years he walked, a father with his son,
Sat among roots in storms, scraped moss
From wooden gates, and counted days remaining.

A fascination grew, to watch a face
Listen to stones, mould mud, cherish a stick.
The marks of their last walk are on the track
He pounds and puffs along. He does his training
In the same, but it's a different, place.

A hare sits upright on a winter hill
Its ears black against the grey of evening.
He drives to fetch his son from his first school.
The moss he scraped today was only moss.
Stones talked only stone. He did his training.

And Light Fading

It's like a de Chirico drawing. The sun going,
A boy on a big grey horse with his bare ankles showing,
A little boy below exclaiming at the hunter's huge feet:
Eyes of saffron calves reflecting yellow light,
Anxious, standing back from the yard gate:
Garish among the ochre fallows
And high bare fields with scooped lavender shadows
A green surprising triangle of winter wheat.

The lane winds up and long. Winter hedgerows
Burn, lemon-green and coral, trap a black bag or sack that blows
Sometimes in a wind above the lane.
Boys and big grey horse and fields and man:
Black plastic like a broken bird, flapping, cracking:
Coloured lane climbing away and turning, narrowing, and light fading.

Edward Thomas in Heaven

Edward, with thinning hair and hooded eyes
Walking in England, haversack sagging, emptied of lies,
Snuffing and rubbing Old Man in the palm of your hand
You smelled an avenue, dark, nameless, without end.

In France, supposing the shell that missed
You and sucked your breath out as it passed
Released your soul according to the doctrine
You disbelieved and were brought up in,
From slaughtered fields to Christian purgatory?
(Assuming your working life, the sad history
You sweated through, and marvellous middens of rural stuff
You piled together were not purgatory enough?)
Are you now a changed person, gay and certain?
Your eyes unhooded, bland windows without a curtain?
Then it would not be heaven. It would be mere loss
To be welcomed in by an assured Edward Thomas.

There must be doubt in heaven, to accommodate him
And others we listen for daily, who were human,
Snuffing and puzzling, which is why we listen.
How shall we recognise the ones we love
If next we see them fitting round God's finger like a glove?
While close-by round him, mistier,
Farther and farther, all the birds
Of Oxfordshire and Gloucestershire
And angels of Breconshire and Hereford
Sing for them, and unimaginable Edward?

The Clapham Elephants

We are two mice looking up at a cupboard of shoes
Smelling a dreaded smell of bigness.
The shoes move. Are grey, dwarfing thoughts.
You look pale too, they appal your small head too.

Round and round go the bony foreheads of the thoughts,
Backwards and forwards, tethered, only inches,
Roundways and sideways in the tent's grey skull.
Soft red mouths
And kind bloodshot eyes inside a grey vertigo,
Caked, cracked, the colour of terrible mornings.

If only they would be still...they seem unable to be still.
Twenty-five elephants swell, retreat, like the sea.
Turds like boxing gloves.
They only look sideways.
Never look at each other, seem resigned
Never to look at anything. Push and sway.

Soon to be ridden by pert girls,
The thoughts become public, make conversation kneeling.
The girls flick sequinned skirts
Again and again over scaly forehead, back,
Their calves in tights tucked behind tatters of ears.

The eyes of the grey thoughts, straddled, look inward.
Later, their dark tent, their huge smell.
Round and round go the grey helpless heads, a grey swell.

Sporting Occasion, Korea

In a flat freezing landscape, the wind cutting their faces,
It was good to reach the homely Northumberland voices
And lorries that howled in the lorry-park, warming up.
Newcastle United had reached the Final of the Cup
And Brigade was flying two men, briefly, home.
A Corporal tuning a Bedford shouted a name
Who came out wiping his hands from the Spare Parts tent
To be rightly unimpressed by an Army stunt.
The other was already dead.
                            Reluctant
To leave the bare clay field, the warm engine noises
And, so far from home, the rooted, sceptical voices,
The messenger walked about in his brother's old officers' coat,
Wind flattening feathers in his Irish officer's hat.

Hidden from lorries in a bombed-out hut
Among broken bricks in the wind a young woman sat
With her breasts pulled out of her clothes, nursing a child.
She made an animal noise, half-whimpered, half-growled.
These were the first bare breasts he had seen
In his life probably, he was about nineteen.
Stopped by the sight, in his thick coat, he half stepped in.
She scuttled away on her heels, in her throat
Making that noise. He stepped quickly out.
Later he lost his coat when shot through it
And later he lost the brother. Still remembers when he'd rather not
Pausing, before going on, to look at a titty:
Feeling lust, embarrassment and, afterwards, pity.

A Walk, a Small Event, a Dream

The walk

Across the empty valley on a morning dark and mustardy
Goosey in his yellow JCB
Is digging a hole for the Doctor from Gloucester,
Pleasant, only neighbour, and devoted gardener. ·

Each day that sheepy hillside gets less sheepy.

Down at the flooded stream
With grasses fighting in it, very green,
We call across his newly planted fence
May we come in?
Gloved, the Doctor cups his ear in hand.
He's holding, with his landlord, conference
Where further little flowerbeds should go.
In tweeds they frown at the beginning snow.

Goosey gouges an Ornamental Pond
Out of an old bog. His pronged bucket
Fiddles to dig it neatly round.
From yellow clay, and green, from under thin
Black topsoil with broken china in it
An oily spring of water dribbles in.
Sandy clay he digs, and handshaped stones
(This is an old place) like old bones.
Rows of levered knobs between his knees, he plays
At driving cranes. New prunus trees
Are planted among the roses, each yellow label
Blown in the mud, illegible.

Tenant and landowner wander on. The hill turns white.

Doctor returns looking quizzical, holding a rabbit
Dangled away from his coat. 'Would you like it?'
Seeming uncertain whether to let the child
See something so warmly limp which had been wild.
With noncommittal eyebrows raised to his hatbrim
Tells respectfully how the rabbit came to him.

The small event

That confident landowner
– All things with wills of their own
Offend his state –
Pulled the rabbit
From its hole and strangled it.
'You eat rabbit?'

Of all the warren
Perhaps the musical one.
With apprehensions finer might we not
Out of a gnat-cloud recognise each gnat?
Thin snow falls
On open eyeballs.
It dangles in mid-run
As though escaping downward.
He did enjoy
Too coarse a triumph
In the blizzard
That landlord.

A dream afterwards

Declaiming against all open hillside gardens
To an unseen audience sitting on a bank,
Walking between the pruned, finical rows
That soon would bloom like florists' windows,
On hoed ground, not boggy, not too much:
Suddenly – very. Sunk to the waist – the chest
– And now the chin. To a friend hidden behind the slope
Examining something, a patina'd privy, a sensible cabbage patch:
I AM DROWNING IN THIS ROSE GARDEN.
Wondering how the mud, soon, will taste,
Innocent earth, after bubbles, over my head.
Relaxing on the pillows of ooze, calm.
Knowing that he will hear and he will come.

Or that he will not hear and will not come.

135

Just Now

A mole on its back with its belly roundly eaten
Like a red jewel on a black velvet cushion
With white clawed feet at the four cushion corners,
Backscratchers, Victorian decorations.
Minutes ago it must have happened, the red so fresh,
Black fur surrounding it so neat and fine.

Along the path a smell of youthful winters
Comes up suddenly from mud and nettlestalks. It goes away
I sniff so hard to make it stay.
A stoat begs up on its toes, almost on my shoes,
Twitching its nose, belly white as light on water.
Trots towards, this morning's definition of Awake.

Awake...Even this world, shrunk
To a child's eyeball, is too much.
And 'What of our common ill – do his works explain?'
Said Austin Clark to A.E. about Yeats.
Said Joyce: 'You chaps are too expansive. I'm expensive.'
Ordered himself a bottle of cheap white wine.

But twenty years of trying should explain,
And simply, why small events like small bones scratch the throat.
Pecking at innards to pick the remembered truth out
Is close-to, jewellers' work. The present, outside on its toes,
Needles into a wall, comes out looking over its shoulder further on,
Packed, already blooded, like the stoat.

LIFE BEFORE DEATH

(1979)

'Is there a life before death?'
(written on a wall)

Dome

Now thin grass on hills is tipped with rust,
Earth cracks in wide-lipped squares and tracks are dust.
Dark leaves on sycamores are whitened by an air
That lifts them gently as it lifts my hair.
My dreamed adventures narrow down to here:
A lonely house with three souls in it that I care
So much for now I wonder how I can
Ever to God or to anyone explain
I feel myself a lost and selfish man
Who am more fortunate than anyone.
My fingers rip off rusty seeds of docks.
Hills stand around impassively as clocks.
Inside the breeze a silence like a dome
Is not homely but it is my home.

For Bruno

*"In truth, I seem mostly to have felt the joys of living;
in recording, thanks to the gift of the Muse, it is the pain."*
                                                    Robert Lowell

You come after school and ask me to write
In the last of a criss-crossed notebook something for you.

Not much I understand and you do not
At six years old is worth attending to
For long. No more meanings in the bright
And windy morning than you found in it
When dawn awoke you.
I tell you this because the gloom
I sometimes sit and write down in my room
May one day startle you.

A gaoler-angel with a bony wrist
Leans on my desk and pouches of amethyst
Colour are under his eyes.
He says he is my guest. He is my guard.

Gladder ones, outside, unpushing,
Rise like birds from morning fields, upgushing...

Swooping like telegraph-wires, a small brown bird
Spilled sound in drops. Its body was a reed
It played by flying with an open throat.
I open mine
And out comes Colonel Carne
Weeping at the crossroads for his men.
Years in a prison-camp he carved a stone
Cross for them. And would not leave
Without it. Guards would not believe
The freed camp said: 'We stay with Colonel Fred.'

Woes
Of the world like gems displayed
In jewel-coloured circles round his eyes.
Never to real trouble a true comrade.
Bruno, the best I do is cross things out
And hear the bird.

To chip beyond the disbelief of guards...

Their jewelled systems crumble round their eyes
And they ask *you*.

As birds, be chary of the word 'Alas'.

*Lt. Col. Carne, V.C. was the commanding officer of the
1st Btn. The Gloucestershire Regiment in Korea, the
whole of which was either killed or captured in April
1951. The cross is now in Gloucester Cathedral.*

Winter Hillside

Wind shrinks an iron rim on our ears.
They trundle ruts of frozen air. The world's not white
But whitey-green, a cloud we are in is whitey-brown
So we can just discern the difference between
Earth and air. And muddy sheep are mist-
Colour too, as though born of the mist.
We bring them broccoli-stumps, they run
Towards us hoping we bring hay,
Scorn the ragged greens, turn away
And range themselves apart in two split wings
To watch. We are alone in the halved field;
One half sheep squadrons, one half us.
We dance with tattered greens, shake them,
Inviting sheep to eat who no more
Understand than we can stand their silent stare,
Motionless, darkling. Lest we disappear
We dance, scatter the greens, feel fools.
Wind smacks our faces wooden. Turning away
From remainders of colours that do not quite exist
A clamp of dark and ice cuts off our laugh
As though it was not (nor was it) ever enough.

Father and Son

In areas of madness softness is:
Huddled in hazels like a King and his Fool,
Sun shaken to pieces by tiers of leaves
Above and, around, brackeny silence:
The world shrunk to a hole, and us inside.

Outside in a globed clearing splendour is:
The sky in a ring of poplars and the floor
Of it white with seeded thistles, white as a ski-run,
Orange pine trees sticking through are rusty docks.

141

My huddle madness, yours a playing is:
We turn the sun on our shoulders like a pip,
Elbow tangles, pushing up to light,
A thin foam of moths around our knees.

The fence – the light – you spread your arms and run
On open stubble; from huddled in shattered brightness
To where enclosed a snow-white open was,
To wind and height itself . . . I feel my mind
Clip, unashamed, to form a hard
Setting for the jewel softness was. It
Held a light. I hold to that.

Snapshots of New York and Hillsdale, N.Y.

At Connolly's on Lexington, you pee on ice-cubes.

Hickory's shaggy bark is undersea growth.
Little scrub maples, grey shining on grey,
Colour the underwoods like a threat of rain.
Huge leaves from higher trees in unseen blue
Drop among them like large animals hopping.
Dry out in humps, sit on their triple points
Humped like animals. When they hop,
When wind comes like a car approaching,
One moves quicker, with better rhythm,
Squats, and is a chipmunk.

ƎϽИAЈUƧMA like Russian, for the rear-view mirror.
Stock-brokers, fortune-tellers, share the first-floor windows.

Clear round ponds with neat placed
Birch-clumps and one marble rock.
Upturned leaves float like paper boats
And grass sings; bright green hoppers
Rise in splashes round the Mohawk's feet.
In chewed doe-skin softer than linen
Among white birch trees he wrinkles eyes

142

At furred hills round as mounds...
THIS IS GOD'S COUNTRY.
'POSTED! Private Property. All persons
Are warned against *Hunting, Fishing, Trapping*
or *Trespassing* hereon for such purpose or
other purpose whatever. Name. R.B. Handelman.
Address: Hillsdale, N.Y.' On each tall tree.

After Queen's, Triboro' Bridge at dusk:
'See that KENT sign? Round there, that's the worst.
They call it Fort Apache.'
The Empire State, soft pinks, greens, crimsons.
A skyline pierced with bright transparencies,
Delicate as wings of dragonflies.

While the Sun Shines

If this is heaven I have the pain of a God that's in it,
Powerless, grieving down at the vanishing minute.
Across the valley a cutter slow as a bug
Cuts a huge hayfield in patterns like nap on a rug.
The bug goes over the hill and its noise fails.
Two downy children hide in a darkness of bales,
In sun and wind on the hilltop to play at jails:
Fed through cracks, stalks stinging the jailer's wrist,
Make-believe bread and water, softly touching his fist,
While over their prison, clouds from behind the scarp
Like smoke from explosions corkscrew suddenly up.

They are new inside their dark; they sing.
I lop old sinewed nettles, willing them to sting.
Children escape, climb up and bring me down.
I fall on stubble, hold their pliant backs,
Go dark in a web of limbs and smell their hair,
Keep their bones from stones and see through cracks
Clouds that spiralled flatten and go elsewhere.

The Odd-job Hunter

Elbows on knees, sitting to be noticed,
Scratching his hangover like an attendant dog,
Puzzled his freedom brings him again this bondage.

Householder sighs, seeing him, sighs,
Says Yes, we've this to do and, Yes,
While children pull at his trousers.

Understanding and half-resenting, half-admiring
His friend the odd-job hunter, the feelings
Cancel each other out and he sees a man

About to walk to the pub to swim in the money
Until he's beached on the bank, and briefly docile.
And another man, himself, who buries his face

Deep in the importunities of his children,
An icy brook that dazes him
And by its speed rejects him so he's left

With beads of cold on his cheek and only
Knowing it's a long way to the sea.

Where You Watching Are

If you indeed look down on us from those high places
Where you unimaginably live – Oh may you not see us
Always dark as the surface of the night-time world!

May you hear nothing but silence, see nothing but darkness,
Where some that you knew presumably still have existence
Of a kind, impenetrably in smoking darkness furled.

Though a wind that blows only sometimes may make a flicker
Start from the smoulder, even a small and pure
Sound may be brought out of darkness by the wind that passes.

May that be all you are able to see and hear!
Do not judge us, only turn towards us
When that wind blows, or there can be no love and no forgiveness.

May you be silent squadrons in silent air,
Ignorant of our squares, our blacked-out cities;
Believing a lonely light that moves is all that lives here,

And ones you loved a glimmer, doubtless, elsewhere,
Or will flicker soon, for we used to glow. Your belief in that is
The wind that raised you where you watching are.

A Single Tree

You ask for more rungs in the ladder I
Built against the solitary tree:
Your legs still short, your brother up already.
So in wind I fix it, and I find
As I lean smoking, back against the tree,
Seagulls driving plovers from their ground,
A picture of two figures, both still young,
Who come across this ladder sagging, rotten,
Leant against a hedge-tree long forgotten,
And wonder at the nearness of each rung;
Watched by their father, trying not to long
To join them or wish again this day
Of wind and gulls and peewits fighting, crying,
Nostalgic falseness in the air, sighing sighing,
Though that was in his mind. So, today,
He takes two cold boys home and gives them food,
Glad he shared with them a single tree
Before they walked without him to the wood.

Don't Forget the Keeper, Sir

Turner, it is hopeless, Art! What you have done
By painting storms is imprison another one.
Your sea-scapes have no soundtrack, their hum
Is air-conditioning and human
Storms and gulfs below them yawn.

A Keeper, straining from his canvas chair,
Held in, framed, by storms no one can hear,
Leaps up, hissing, beckons me with a stab
At the picture he sat by: '*It has no* HULL,
That boat!' The absence has driven a hole
In his peace, he loathes that storm-tossed blob
And sits to cover his canvas with a storm
Crushed back inside his frame of uniform,
Windowless, under neon. While, outside, the river
Endlessly marries dirty light and water,
Bound for honeymoon and salt absolution
He sweats among the creak of waters you have frozen.

A Great Gale, 1976

A hairy dog, house-size,
snuffled and licked at windows.
Dark aircraft squadrons
trod on each others' roaring.
Roof-tiles flapped like
hinged cat-windows and trees
tipped, drowned in wind,
were levered lids of earth,
showed yellow root-rocks.

That was home. At Maidstone
'Beware Guard Dogs'. On
the great hall table was

146

a cosh, with a leather wrist-thong.
'Mr Lowell is not here.'
Telephoned: 'I – forgot.
Shall I come to you?
A thousand pardons...'
I went to him, in London.

Outside the Tate the car
lifted, a tin rag.
A dark house, a red
cliff...Two bare feet,
a tousle, resumed position
prone under one bare bulb
on the bed, a silhouette
among versions of versions of poems:
'Read this. Better than Wyatt?'

Did *sortes Virgilianae*
from the Loeb requiring
me to translate, using
the crib himself – a competitor:
'Berryman wanted to be
better than Homer'...Supine,
a match between himself
and himself, he ran to return
his own service: 'Met a man

looked like Hitler. Asked him
"Why didn't you like Speer?"
"He dressed too well"...'
Likeable, ill, logical
as wind. The wind came in
the hollow house. He talked
faster. Left a Hiroshima
imprint on the bed
among versions of versions

to show – in a room like a mind –
treasures of furniture trapped
wind was screaming round
like thoughts in a skull piling
on top, on top...I held

147

my ears…He looked behind
in courteous wonder,
half-innocent, like wind on
trees toppled over.

Breakfast in Italy

Your words have gaps round, they work, John.
You may be glad to hear so, Berryman,
If you hear where you have gone.
You hoped they might. And jumped to darkness.

In Italy you said: 'Do you drink whisky?'
At 9 a.m. I answered, Yes,
Not now. Your glass
The colour of tea, milkless.

Afraid, all week I fled the continents of sweat
With white encrusted coasts on your alpaca jacket;
Propped by acolytes, your maniac howl
At parties, I called a Soul Commercial.

It sounded so. Now at a pavement café
Your whisky in a tea
Glass you half entrap me for a tale
About the lie you made of three

Lives, one yours, for sake
Of love. Through memories you blink
At morning traffic. I am a lost
Guest pretending to be host.

You are clear, inside a blurred ghost.
'So' (you bless the passers), now I *drink*!
But wild *horses* wouldn't make
Me tell a *lie*!' Hoisted

Over the street to buy your airline ticket
Suddenly you turned and kissed me, hard.
I feel your dreadful beard,
Even now ... You learned such speed,

John, when you wrote. Maybe a good
Man too, God knows.
As a saint then, John, you were odd
And quick to mark. Cunning it was,

By grasp to name a trouble shared,
And generous. One who doubted
Now no word against you hears...
Self-pity for the tribe you wrote, and showed.

Ivor Gurney

To cast out a shout of love to a far
Country, long loved, and be given bare
Silence, and cold unhonouring there.   (I.G.)

I, Fortunatus, twang my string
Outside the Institution where you stood
      In line for food,
   And try to send a ray of sound
Much too late to cross the grass and touch
      A solitude,

   A hurt as great as any man
Has had, which haunts, because you wrote it down.
      No man is mad,
   Though maddened in the end,
Who writes such clear, such terrible and justified
      Complaints to God

   They haunt the day, this February
Light, yellow and green; the way I see
      Black rooks discuss
   New sun, on outer twigs, and keep
So tight to the shape of the tree – armorial birds
      On a field of skies

You cast out such a shout of love to,
That love itself stood back, dismayed...Escaped
    From hospital
  You stole and ate a pound of butter
Straight from the paper. The widow of your brother
    Shudders still

  In Gloucester: 'How could a man *do* that!'
Hunger unappeasable was put away
    For fifteen years
  Until it starved. And there was mud,
Too, on your clothes, from lying in fields to stare
    Back at stars...

  Exalter of every shift of sky
By the end you would not raise your eyes:
    'I don't know
  About sunsets, never see them now.'
Where was the light, for fifteen years, for you?
    Today the slow

  Turning of seasons you could no longer
Bear to notice, Fortunatus watches
    With your eyes
  That later blurred over copies and copies
Of verses, over and over...Such desolation
    Also stays.

  What God controls a surly ghost
That watched itself diminish while it lived?
    Though the work
  Be worship now, and you are best
At last, who worshipped all there was and lost
    It, lost it
  Till you could not look?

Spoleto 1967

'Why are Academic poets
so goddam intemperate!'
said robed Allen Ginsberg. Why
do poets pay homage
to old Ezra Pound,
including Allen? I was
hungry. Beneath the TV lights
Mr Pound, pale, blinking,
silent, as it was
rumoured he had been
for years, a queue
forming of Great Poets
culled for the Festival, I
ordered a pizza.
From the queue he turned
and watched the pizza
from my hand to my
mouth, up and down;
his pale face up
and down, with the pizza.
Why
did I not offer
him some, at the head
of the queue of his
pilgrims? What
could silent, long suffering
Ezra have done but snub me?
Fame intervened, poets
should not have queued.

I should have offered.

'A few still believe in heavenly reunions'

Philip Toynbee

If you saw five birds on a wire and I saw three
I would count again and stay uncertain. Certainty
(Nor do I want it much) is not my *forte*.
It came unbidden. I sat in the roots of a tree,
A square of hospital window illumined behind me:

A choiring of angels? A clear-skied thunderclap?
A Sisyphus heave, heave, of concentration?
A 'mystical experience', at least, a leap
Into the fifth, ninth, whatever it is, dimension?
Simpler than that. A tank of loss filled up,

Faster than I could think or breathe, with reassurance.
A sufficient, unnoticeable filling, as the heart
Pumps unnoticed, so this seemed the thought
That thinks itself, the pure intelligence
Saint John describes as there before the start.

Not to be found by brains, or loins – or hearts;
Not to be found at all, it being there.
In pain, or in mere distraction, when the mind permits
Its parts free action, they come winging back, cohere.
You lose yourself; it calls out – 'We are here.'

As at those moments when unconsciously
We do some task, blankly looking out at bush or tree
The thinnest skin is lifted from our eye –
Black outer twigs, a lichen bole of green, cinnamon centre,
And we see...? Nothing is certain, except that we die

And even that doesn't perfectly answer the question.
Certainly untrue one day a lucky man is sent a
Hopeful message down from deaf, dumb heaven.
I sat in the roots of a tree and went a
Journey nowhere, in my skin. It was reunion.

I no more doubt it than I doubt my feet.
It is not possible to *think* the Paraclete.
'A few'...No, there are more, though few of us can bear
The speed. Even there, in charged air
I heard my mind slam, an iron gate.

Though what had flashed flies, easily, in and out.

News from Gloucestershire

This snow, thaw, frost, thaw and rain
Has bitten great gaps in the old limestone
Walls that summer visitors delighted in:
Dark grey, with rusty orange and sky-grey lichen
And mosses green as cress; they caught the sun
Pink in the morning and, white under the moon,
Shadowed the fox. They have fallen down,

Nor will be, nor should be, built again,
Fences being cheaper; they are done
That were my passion. Foxes' navigation, weasels' run,
Skilful catchers of every light, they open
Like graves, a jumble of yellow bone
That tractors ridy away. Visitors from the town
May vaguely remark an absence, travel on.

The thud, thud, is fence-posts going in.

The Dead

Do this morning the dead, turned inwards towards brightness,
Over their shoulders feel pictures of living arrive?
Recall the old tenderness of dusky, windswept mornings,
Overgrown verges bent under weight of sky,
Everything blackish, solid, with clear-cut edges
And birds splashing like fish in soaking hedges?

Why else do they seem to turn to us today?
For now they know we do not know we relish
The end of love, evaporation of children,
While we enjoy them, love our own death even;

That melancholy is our atmosphere. Like autumns
We watch our own departing...We must like it.

The only way to lose regret, to die?

The road shines wet, the sky is dead, the hairy hedges
Are blackest at this season. As though they think
The passer knows some answer, sheep huddle and watch
Him turn the corner, move their heads as one. (When he peers
Behind he sees them watch a while his disappearance.)
Why do the dead come winging in, our melancholies
Lost on them, above a hedge so black, now, against greyness,
Making the air go still? They push at our confinement,
Soft as breath; yearn for sadness like a lost refinement.

Simile

Just as the house For Sale you did not buy

(not to choose it you try it on in your mind
so in a sense you live there)

inhibits further choices

(when was it I lived in the house with a privy
and crooked damson tree that scraped the window
that was the place not this one)

so does the idea coming late at night

(fleshed in surprising rhythms and natural colours
connections clear as avenues leading off
as in the formal park-scape of a chateau
towards a triumphant gravelled logical centre
gone when you sit to write it in the morning)

prevent all day another unbidden arrival.

After Reading the Life
of Arthur McMurrough Kavanagh 1831-1889

An Arab on the bank of the Nile
Watched him roll overboard, round
As a pebble, a human whale

That sank. Arab ululation warned
His Irish brothers. He was drowned
Unconscious; no one mentioned this;

Gentlemen, trained not to notice
(As he trained Prince, his pony-hound
To drag his body round the hall)

That he was armless, legless.
Though he mentions, coolly, the cactus
In Albania, that held his fall

Down the face of a precipice,
Strapped to his horse, helpless;
How mountain climbers cut him loose:

'There is something peculiarly exciting
To the nerves, in looking
Down an abyss, and going

Over into it...' A young whale
At Bergen stood on its tail
To see him, another doomed species.

Rough-rider, shooter – no one says
How he managed. Influential Member,
His yacht at Westminster,

'Landlord who never raises the rent.
Who props the tottering tenant.'
Loud applause. Renewed cheers...

Weeks later the cheerers had him out
Of Parliament, lit delighted bonfires
Round his gate...'I do not think that

Forty of my fellows gave me the vote.
Passing the rest of my life among
Them – almost more than I can do.'

Who judged disputes in open air
Under his oak, with his ape, his bear;
Who began by tying his dog to a cart

Till cousins thought his trunk was fun:
'I have always felt, my dear,
How hollow was the ground we stood upon.'

Looking down a dizzy abyss and going
Over into it. Doomed as the blue
Whale, as game he shot.

Vespers, and Notices, at Prinknash Abbey

It's always the human
catches the attention
first: the shaven crown
of the Master of Ceremonies
who glides his feet,
who slides them flat
under his gown.
He must practise.
He turns as though he rounds a corner
to catch his swirl in a mirror.

Each voice
blends with another, smoothly. Calm
is surprising as we come
in late from an autumn
afternoon already
calm enough. There is more
here. Caught in a theatre
of calm we bow together.
The old formula,
clothes, candles, Sion,
Melchisedec, Aaron...
The children
receive the drip of names
impassively, the formality
they seek in games.

I would give them a formula
if I could, a glide
to reach the other side
of ice...Why not?
                    THE BIRD
PARK 15 Yards → THE FARM SHOP
– that soundless glide
formal as leaves that drip
in salmon light –
THE CEMETERY (*No through road*).

Gardening

Impatient with his task, dreading the sound
Of his own voice, which had become hypnotic,
He went to the garden to dig, to take
Small green weeds out of the wet ground.
The evening was bright and clear, the clouds high,
Thin blue was fading gradually to green
With bands of orange, an early owl was screaming.
And he thought of Father Howell's saintly manner
Of raising his arms and calling angels down
As though he felt them coming; of Father Reilly,
Twenty-five years in England, son of Fermanagh,
His voice remaining impenetrable as Swahili
Reading the Gospel in chapel, every word
Against his palate crashed and splintered;
A polite congregation dreaming inaudible words, dreaming
Of peace and help. And peace and help coming.
For of the congregation he was one,
There to acknowledge their own, and the world's, pain.

Digging, the high sky losing its last green,
He could think for the moment of no other way to do this –
A thin old priest inviting angels down
Because their help was needed, with upturned face;
And unconsciously putting eloquence back in its place
A round practical man with a swallowed voice –
Having come to the end of himself and the sound of his own.

Beyond Decoration

Stalled, in the middle of a rented room,
The couple who own it quarrelling in the yard
Outside, about which shade of *Snowcem*
They should use. (From the bed I'd heard
Her say she liked me in my dressing-gown
And heard her husband's grunt of irritation.

Some ladies like sad men who are alone.)
But I am stalled, and sad is not the word.
Go out I cannot, nor can I stay in,
Becalmed mid-carpet, breathless, on the road
To nowhere and the road has petered out.
This was twenty years ago, and bad as that.
I must have moved at last, for I knelt down,
Which I had not done before, nor thought I should.
It would not be exact to say I prayed;
What for? The one I wanted there was dead.
All I could do was kneel and so I did.
At once I entered dark so vast and warm
I wondered it could fit inside the room
When I looked round. The road I had to walk down
Was still there. From that moment it was mean
Beyond my strength to doubt what I had seen:
A heat at the heart of dark, so plainly shown,
A bowl, of two cupped hands, in which a pain
That filled a room could be engulfed and drown
And yet, for truth is in the bowl, remain...
Today I thought it time to write this down,
Beyond decoration, humble, in plain rhyme,
As clear as I could, and as truthful, which I have done.

The Moon in Charge

Tonight a gale that scattered ships like grass
Makes twigs twitch. Fields stay flat
Under winds arrived from seas they dug
Keel-deep, made white
Panes in the wheel-house hiss like pans...

The moon, presiding also over green turmoil
Appears to skid and stop, in a gold piazza of
Pigeons sleeping, dreaming of feather-massage:
As a girl, shoving through crowds towards her lover,
Who stands alone in a quiet square,
When she sees him slows,
Stops, remembers, with the strange half-smile of ancient statues.

159

A girl in a white robe stands and waits
On moon-stilled grass with long bare feet and walks no further,
However across the pale fields I call.

Sun Overcast

When brightness leaves the trees they seem to fall
Backwards, deprived of shadows, then rise again in a cool
Diminishment of waiting, solider still.

                                   Which it is possible
Is what they mean whom death makes audible
Beyond our ears and, I feel, as simple.

Elder

Feigns dead in winter, none lives better.
Chewed by cattle springs up stronger; an odd
Personal smell and unlovable skin;
Straight shoots like organ pipes in cigarette paper.
No nursery man would sell you an
Elder – 'not bush, not tree, not bad, not good'.
Judas was surely a fragile man
To hang himself from this – 'God's stinking tree'.

In summer juggles flower-plates in air,
Creamy as cumulus, and berries, each a weasel's eye
Of light. Pretends it's unburnable
(Who burns it sees the Devil), cringes, hides a soul
Of cream plates, purple fruits in a rattle
Of bones. A good example.

Dandelion

Sure as a soldier to find the best place,
Dig down deep and then spread out
A green, split groundsheet; a coarse, cheerful face,
Never fresh yellow, on a deceptive neck
Staffed with reinforcements; yellow job soon done,
Consolidates, constructs a startling wig
As decoy for the winds to take;
Sticks the fuzz aboveground, waits.
Platoons of sons are whirled away to dig...

Stiff bald fathers with coarse-pored pates
See to wider billets for their groundsheets.

Memory

Have pity on your upstart,
Lord, when he opens his heart
to try to share the weight of
the burden all men alive
carry, which is baffled love.

For him, when he was callow,
you gave the best of gifts to,
Morfudd. A smell of thunder
brings her close, or thoughts of her.

Dry till now, a swallow's wing
dips into its first washing
as rains on leaved branches fill
air with the smell of metal
– as when you on Eden's hill
forged man, of dust and spittle.
Then, like a beast on a spring-
trap, man stepped on suffering...

161

A wall-haunting weasel caught
in a gin cannot forget
the ways that brought him to it,
Lord. A man remembers all
his twistings. Rain, and rain-smell
of iron in air, and wings
(arguings and twitterings
have dared inside the window;
he stays still in case they go)
newly arrived from the south
make him remember a mouth
loved, but never kissed enough,
Morfudd, who was his glory,
waiting – he remembers he
half-feared to burn entirely...

Is it our fleshly presence
gets in the way of a sense
of a heat we know is there
but are not built to endure
– as we stare up at a star?

If so, what are you up to,
Lord, must all love be for you?
A man, with the chance again,
should bend to the wind, as rain
taking its shape from the air
hurtles to earth, its pleasure,
so should he go, and be with,
entirely, his Morfudd...

Our body is our burden,
it cannot grow in the garden,
sleep, and then grow, in season
innocently, and children
must bend to a shape they learn
as this is bent to a rhyme
of bright Dafydd ap Gwilym
to make out of air a form
for Morfudd, for memory
dropped from the leaves of a tree...

Look up – the swallows have gone.
The spittle and dust half-done,
their mud-shape they abandon
when he moves. – He cries out 'Fly
to Morfudd, tell her memory
like a trap has enclosed me
today, and say I am glad.
I do not struggle inside.
Morfudd will guess why rain-scent
of iron fills his present
who moved till swallows flew,
whose bulk obscures the window
until, like her, he has no
form to be caught, or shadow.'

On Giglio

for Lynn and Frank MacShane

We climb above the green domes where we stay,
the American-built dream-house on a dry
island, accessible only by sea –
or by falling down this bed of a winter
torrent, ripped, for half an hour
from the dirt road high above. While climbing
we hear from a thicket a sighing
encouragement and a mule slides, sideways-on,
the man behind it pretending a grin
which is only teeth. We show him ours.
                                    . . . At Rosdahan
in Ireland Pat O'Keefe sitting regarding
the loneliest, mildest, fuschia-hung
stretch of the south Kerry shore where he kept
an old donkey, a sheep or two, and mostly slept
to dream of a small tobacconist's shop in Dublin.
'Here? Just look at it! Ah, the tedium . . .'
We are the mule-man's dream,
maybe he thinks we see him tethered
to his burning island like a lizard.

163

He is a dream of ours, a dream of rhythm
tied to gathering stuff as our ancestors might.
Both dreams, as dreams go, right
enough as the dreams awkwardly pass
on a torrent-bed made awkward for the feet
of a mountain mule by the mile-long plastic pink
American pipe meant to bring water to drink,
one day, at the green-domed house.
There never will be water in the pipe...
Parched inhabitants will see to that.
We sweat, scratched, to the top.
Find the car with its boot like an envelope
flap almost tenderly levered open
and the spare can, like a small tax, taken
to pay for the dream of rhythm
and the dream we are of a small tobacconist's shop.

Pilgrims

We pray to a picture. A candle lit,
Before the Madonna del Parto by Piero,
To give you an easy birth and healthy baby.
I believe in it, as I believe the green
Grapes outside will grow unless it hails.

Borris House, Co. Carlow

Ancestor-hunting: an interest as sudden
As middle age. As though I thought a chain
Of farmers, post office keepers, castle holders,
Bog kings, knackers, farmers' workers, traitors,
Clanked at my heel. And I did find one

Great-grandfather an old grandee or a great
Liar...French Jacobins making thought a thing to fear
What did they do, those summits of others' labour
Behind high walls, the nearest speakable neighbour
Sodden, impassable Irish miles away? In 'Ninety Eight

Some flogged the blacksmiths; busy, essential men
With a ring of lingering magic round their craft.
Here ten were chained to the wine-cellar walls in dark
– The benches they sat on crumble away to cork –
And out of the ten, for death, one was chosen.

Perhaps he had made pikes for the Rebellion.
Perhaps not. Examples must be made, possessions held.
Perhaps. In recent years, over a bottle of wine,
The Rate Assessor faced the heir, his business done:
'Your ancestor' he said, 'killed one of mine...'

That was a just fight, cruelly put down.
The wall still stands, the length of the little town,
Whichever side of it, twenty years later, he was born
An embattled grandee, or great liar. Not a man
But knows both titles privately his own.

For C.E.K.

I would if I could write new words for women
because of you.
I never dreamed you in a flour-caked apron.
Though you may think so.
I never dreamed you, either, a kneeling figure
cleaning the nose of a dying rabbit,
feeding it with your fingers, day after day –
the children's Flopsie. (Seen from the corner of the eye
a tolerated creature becomes an enlarging habit,
a separation, a world, determined; its white
glowed on the grass at night, a spectral light,
a dumpish dignity.) We took it to be anaesthetised to death,

165

unsaveable. I would have left it with the vet.
You held it, smiling. In your hands its breath
gentled, its rasping rhythm slowed and – 'Flopsie flopped'
I might have wished to say, but no –
into the white element she seemed to go,
soundlessly to melt, like snow in snow,
dignified, determined. This I saw because of you,
among horse-douches, rabies posters. Her breathing stopped,
you said (to the rabbit) 'There', removed your hand,
still smiling...Nothing there I cannot understand.
There may be things that I have falsely dreamed,
but not from you. The moment seemed,
and was, as moments with you sometimes are, all I waking
want: a fellow-soul, surprising. Not an 'us'.
Another, a separation, taking
its own line;
a fellow-man – a space between us glows, miraculous –
who is not one.

Spring Arrival

Morning looks out at the sodden air,
having travelled all night, as through
the steamed-up windows of a foreign café,
watching shoes of a kind not sold at home
heavy with destinations on rain-dark pavements,
drinking unfamiliar chocolate, tasting
instead of bread a half-sweet roll...
an underwater, suspended, arrival feeling; buds
in the caves of their crinkled scarves sip
their first cold moisture, half-observing
the foreign traffic of shouting birds.

Bread-and-Butter Letter

'Ben Jonson his best piece of poetry'   (of his son)

You made me a tick in the rich fur of the world.
Good God, what could have been bald is various!
Dropping red berries under the nettled footbridge,
On our bellies to watch, relieved as you when they re-emerged,
Or some; our faces almost touching the muddy water,
Around us the fur crackled, sparked, with bits of God,
Hidden for safety in what is always there...

No one can loon alone, not to that purpose. You
Were the poetry, I was born your son
In fur the height of your shoulder.
To be born into life before death a second time!
No murder can change it, only I can.
Though saved I may be by the visit
I cannot return –
                        Your grateful guest.

Praying

As lark ascending
Ending in air
Sings its song there,
If sounds I am sending
Don't go anywhere
I seem not to care

After singing the lark
Drops back to the ground.
I cover the dark
With the palm of a hand
As horses in fields suddenly stop
Their gallop at a horizon and crop.

Seal

As often, behind the ribs, like a seal
Caught in an undertow, the heart dips,
Lurches in broken seas, in turmoil.

But you, seal in the cove, you roll
In seas twice the height of yourself,
Your polished back, greyer than sky

Curves with the rondure of sea
And dives; to a calm palace of glass
To watch the anger from under?

An absence where you were. No creature
Is anywhere so at home as you are...
From black rocks your armour

Is only roundness, shining. Dark-helmeted bather,
Not eating, enjoying, again you are there,
A static snout, in turmoil. 'See

I am round as waves and world. The
Warmth of cold. Anywhere
Else I bark and slither. Master
Of sea. No. The sea my twin.
Sea is the love I am in.'

Illness

At times it is good to be cold and ill and small
As things that in a bare world have no rest
From owl and weasel, in a cold world no nest:
For one foot lifted to be a victory, a smile
Or word an imitation word, a smile remembered
From days before the silences began
To ring and ripple and enclose us, settle down
As moss settles and closes round a stone.

Then earth at last can bear us who were crude
Stepping lightly past a frozen bird.
Earth approves our weight because enfeebled we go gently
Past lichens paler green than sky, cold stones
Puffing powder-colour through at our bones,
And on our skins the weightless dead try breathing circumspectly.

Air

Ocean-skin can cream and curdle
Like a leaden custard stirred from below.
Spray-spikes can grow out of calm
And high drowning greens, drawn by moons.

So can air, with knobs and yieldings, drown.

To walk through air as though it has no surface
Is to be ill from smallness.

No fungus-stump, or house
Stones that turn to moss,
Calls change loss.
But how can any element console
A man, always on fire,
Who calls ash failure?

Tell him, oh,
There is no disaster
And no dove! In a shoal
Of powers that move as one
Fish, that scatters, reforms
– A storm within storms –
He is, a Mariner of air

Who thinks himself a lone fish there.

PRESENCES: NEW POEMS

(1987)

A Small World

Fair and frail, declined into a drinker,
Pabulum for the Gloucestershire social worker,
Slumped in a pub, met a magical Lurgan tinker
(Drinker himself) who declined into her Keeper,

Or rose, for he was a kind one. Her demands so swelled
He turned on her, 'Woman! You want the *world*!'
But he shopped for her bottles and pills and, magical, found
One – an atlas-globe; it was Antarctica, white and round

Thrown among roadside grasses and spurted gravel that caught
His incredulous poacher's eye and, quick, it went under his coat.
Returning with clinking bagfuls he dumped them, 'There.
But here's what you really wanted!' Now her stare

Released from globe and from bottles focused on him
At last: 'Sometimes – it is good to be with you, Tom.'
Here was a breaking indeed! As though Antarctica
Should melt, had melted her. Once more he wrestled her despair:

'In the Battle of Life there is no conscientious objector'
He scrawled in chalk above her fire. But she was gone too far
In ice, and ice too far in her.
She found the end she sought for, frail and fair,

Dead among roadside grasses, where he could not find her.
Bitter the taste of all he drank, although, (his turn to stare),
Somewhere in every glass an unaccustomed flavour:
The words she had said of her world when he gave it to her.

Late Acknowledgement

Elizabeth Pritchard, Elizabeth Pritchard, Liz,
We never know whom we shall miss.
Some deaths leave a gap that heals over
But others leave presences.

Last summer I teased when you filled every corner
With jugs of wild grasses
And froze to a statue under our tentative swallows.
But later when scything the grasses
It was your everywhere reverent vases
I saw, not the rankness I cut.
And in bird-empty wind when I walk on the swallows' messes
Crusting the floor of the shed still, even in winter,
It is never the birds I remember
But you, Elizabeth.

Even the pebbles you put to guard willow-herb seedlings
I find that I nod to, whether I want them or not,
As though the degree of your care for the small and abandoned
And tentative, lingers, a seedling you planted.

You, who called yourself dotty, a typical dotty lone woman,
Unlucky in love, and I half-agreed and agree;
Though Elizabeth Pritchard,
Still puzzled and not understanding
Enough, when I think how I'd like to
Swing you up high to the mirror,
As grown-ups with children, a hand under each elbow,
To show you, triumphant, too late now,
The presence you are,
It is you that holds me.

Farmworker

Manhandled haybales not so yellow
As her hair, careful to leave a
Way for the nested swallow.
No stranger knocking the door
Of her stone nest received an answer:
Her back to the window she stayed in her chair.

At walking-pace she rode her tractor
Like an old horse, you could follow
On foot her slumped back, her world
Of foxed perspex, watch the field
Barely grow in her windscreen,
Hedges come to attention, thorn by thorn.

For her to fail is like the season
Failing. Like a swallow, with less hesitation,
With no pause on a wire, she is gone.
Hedges lie doggo,
Hoping to die where they are,
To suffer birds and not have to answer.

Ars est celare artem

homage to Louis MacNeice

Wish me luck blackbird, in *appogiature* from roof-top.
Whether the tune is mating or fighting or stating the joint is
Yours as far as a bird can sing, it sounds like praises
Duly delivered, that roofs have aerials, that rain can stop.

Wish me luck worm, whose moment has come, now looking absurd
In the beak of the blackbird. You were enjoying your oozes,
Content, and are now in mid-air, headed for darker places.
Luck to me, tabby, attentively marking the arc of the blackbird.

Wish me luck lovers on fire, alight with your first undressing,
And Darby and Joan, yawning and putting the tea on;
The lonely, the grief-struck, every imperfect one,
All the dismayed. Here one of your number is asking the blessing

Of eloquence, speed, Muse's assistance (whatever the phrase is –
We have to be quick for cat will have bird and bird has the worm
And worm will get all, Darby and Joan and those lovers so warm)
For that poet's cool music, whose love for the various,

Seen from an angle, made his notes for it natural
(Weather-eye cocked for a bolt from the innocent blue)
As those of this blackbird who sings while he can, and all should do.
For whom and for why should a sky so full stay still?

Birth of Middle Age

As slowly they collapse
with strokes, cancers, booze,
the ones who dandled us,
our warm life falls apart,
an eggshell; what comes out
is us, at best cadet
wrinklies, fledgling gnarled persons.

We can't face up to that,
not now! At every corner
the bullying past, not the future,
tortures with imperfections
in how we used our rations
of love and insight when
we lived in albumen.

I look along the lane
where I first dandled one
and we first lived together

(every house since then
nearer harsh weather)
and want my ration back

and hear the eggshell crack.

Walmer Castle

Leaves of summer
Strong and green
That gusts have strewn
Across his lawn
A lower wind
Sweeps in a line
Now, neat as a windscreen-
Wiper, on.
Wellington here
Asleep in his chair
Whisped his last breath
Into east Kent air.
(His mask after death
With no false teeth in
Is unsparing, unkind.)

Dismissive, that wind
Rolls summer, a window-blind,
Up. I see out
To a yew-sheltered clearing.
See where I sit
A father with sons
Both nearly grown
Now, thinking of bronze
Masks and my own
Life, the unsparing
Wind of it.
Watching the season
Sweep round our feet
Cross as a barman
Impatient to shut.

Politics

Words are moles, they tunnel underground,
Your best one 'progress', mine (unspoken) 'light'
Burrowed towards, which you might call retreat.
We stand in silence, failing to understand
Even our silences: friends, and desperate
On your last morning here, looking across at land
You farmed for years, and painted, a breath
Of green on its brown, an exhalation, after snow.
Old Communist – 'I want to paint what's *underneath*
Those hills. I don't want light' –
You break our silence with my word unsaid.
It throws its hillock like a barricade.

Birthday Visit

Words in air heard
Because they were spoken aloud
When he did not mean to speak
Suspend themselves like smoke
While he visits a grave
And thinks of her alive
Of course with the sense we have
That death is impossible
And marvels again at the girl-
Courage trapeze-grace
That launches itself in space
Because it likes a face.

The world could not go on
Without the valour of women.

A thin young man rufous
Poor with faults enough
She trusted with her life
Older moves to Mary's
Church and makes to leave.
Is halted. He can hear
The words cleansed of grief
She made him capable of
As though she stood there
'God, you were brave!'
An admiration pure
Involuntary as a cough.

A Father Reorganises

Loss of a companion
Grown from his place
Is inevitable, obvious.
But fog lets hedges drip
Tearfully into brown
Mulch which is their loss
Of summer and day shrinks
To fifteen yards across.
Bearded with fog-tears sheep
Huddle and blink, as he blinks
At inevitable loss.

He pushes the white circle
And fog reveals identical
Spirographs, a burning glass
Whose rim is indeterminate
But bright
Almost to burning is
The empty centre of it,
A glass that magnifies
His loss to such a size
He sees it ludicrous,
So bends to put his face,

Fraternal, sympathetic,
Nearer summer's wreckage:
On his neck
A fog-tear smashes
Not quite ice.
He keeps it there because
Drips and neck connect:
For icy execution
Of regret: for a connection
With hedge, fog, grace
Of a shorn season and his own.
Or he hopes it is.

Prayer in Middle Age

God, grant good manners and sobriety
To one who fears that he may sit all day
Your gift to him made useless, with the knock
Reproachful behind one eyeball of last night's whisky.
Nor splendour nor forgiveness does he ask –
These words he says in darkness before daybreak –
Only, sober, to be as he is full glass in hand,
Passably kind to people he cannot stand.
Not for a salve, nor for anyone else's sake,
He asks for a kit of manners; a mask
For what he feels increasingly, dislike.

Heysel Stadium 1985

How could we believe that
A secular ritual
Childish Cup Final
Could help us forget
What we know of the human

Forty years after Belsen
Undreamed by John Skelton?
Christe eleison.
Hawthorn laburnum
Serenely not human
Drip over the wall.
Spring going on
Detached and professional
As a policeman
Unhearing a criminal
Pleading for pardon.
As adults with children
Who become nuisances
Turn to each other,
As policeman to pleas
From a desperate prisoner
'You should have thought
Of that when you did it'
Hawthorn laburnum
Are staring straight at us
However we plead with them
To let us in.
And rhyming the shame
Of it need never finish.
With loss we are drunken –
'Ora pro nobish'? –
And who to forgive us?
Ora pro nobis.
Dona nobis pacem.

Token

When we examine skies
For hopeful messages
Although their texture is
Today grey leather
There seems a decoration
Punched in the leather
A distant moving pattern
An axe-head bird-formation.

Or it is those shadows
Floating on our eyes
That flatter emptiness.
Gentling down the stages,
Unseen steps of air,
The sky blank again,
There rocks a token, a
Sky-boat breastfeather.

Drifts

(i)

Sheep go dark
In a noise of squadrons.

Morning is sculpted ears
Preening swans' necks
Over the burst snowplough.

Sheep in ice-mail
Butting the hay-bringer.
Tear at bales
Drool bale-string.

This will pass:
A jewelled thaw
And on the plain –
Drowned cattle.

The Spring?
The Future?
A tinkling rhythm of snows, thaws,
'Progress',
That child's play?
At five
Mandelstam wept at the word,
'Its whiff of evil'.

All is a drift
We are in.

No Spring else.

Or only clockwork.

(ii)

Drifts like funeral cards
Have black deckled edges.
Air off-white
With breathed-up whiteness
Cannot lift.

You sit in a shawl staring
Beyond all thought of snow or melt.
Your window useless.
Stare at a wall instead
With eyes as pretty
Again as when your brothers
Died in Flanders, in Gallipoli.
You muddle up their names,
You stare, unanguished,
And remember – not much,

As though a last
White silence to wait through
And no thaw,
A shawl, you pull it round your shoulders,
A last drift.

(iii)

One snowploughed road is clear. Clear to the future?
A night to risk elsewhere.
Two white gaps in a white bank in white fog.
I take the wrong one,
A frozen Cresta cup
To another car, dead in a drift,
Corking the ice-run.
'Well – the *booger*!'
Snow-dazed he turns a key which opens nothing.
I dig in the dark,
Give a last shove without hope –
A sudden connection –
He flips away in blackness like a fish.

Alone, to the vanished tail-lights,
(Somewhere, banging away, a beat of myth),
'How many drifts of calendar pages
Brought me to this icy fastness
And no colleagues?'

Back under lights at last, shaken beyond reason,
(Some roads are cleared but we are in a fist)
Still deafened by that thorough bass somewhere,
I slowly hear you talking of your future,
First marks of adolescence on your face,
Strain lines, pores blocked,
And see the ice-runs,
Mistaken lanes, green Himalayas, dust-bowls
In your face.
The same long epic to an icy fastness,
Stalled.
We must be dazed by whiteness.

I turn the key to speak, but –
'Well – the *booger!*' –

Connection made, it vanishes, a fish.

Beside the Bed

Patient bones in a sack,
Barely a mound beneath
The sheet, your rasping breath
Should give me childhood back:
Our quiet pictures when
You were all I knew.
Instead, on screen,
Something I never called you,
A girl I never saw
Appears, Agnes O'Keefe,
And your brothers, dead in a war
Three generations ago,
Laughing, welcoming you,
As though this was the life
You needed to return to,
And I an interlude
Between that childhood grief
And brothers who understood
Agnes...little Agnes.
Not my childhood, yours.
But how did that projectionist
With unimagined archive
Film arrive?
You may have expected this,
As patient bones of a tree
Wrapped in a white mist
Are suddenly touched by sun,
Given colours again,
Seem to expect no less.

Snowdrops

White grapnels pin our snowdrifts down,
Which shrink, humiliated. What they scorn
They decorate when safely through, their open
Petals feign apology. But on
   A disproportionate strength for a low floating flower.

We sentimentalise, 'the last of winter',
Which for us is never. In easy green,
A drift unworthy competition,
They yellow and go down. Their season
   Ours, darkness, ice, to pierce and float low over.

Nature Poet

1. *Voices*

Peering for clues in dust on a brown moth's wings,
Touching white doors and greening stones in a wall.
Pondering lichen shapes and lines in his nail,
He liked all the people he could and, more than is usual,
Cherished his dead, thought often of them, because they were still.

But bewildered he was, more and more: enamoured of Things
Because they contained a patience and a waiting.
His voices clamoured for clarity: 'All would be easing
If only you'd stop watching trees. Their way of standing'
His voices insisted, 'is their way of teasing.'

He bad-temperedly argued; the voices were his soul,
Nine-cheerful-tenths of it, and gazing got him nowhere;
Stroking the hair of barley, hanging on to a chair
As though it contained a vision carpentered from air,
Left him standing, led him to idleness and despair.

Yet he could not let go, could not. Inside that wall,
In wings of moths, in lists of patient Things he detected mercy
Wafting, like a smell. His voices had their say.
He companionably stared across horizonless grey,
His children fading, his dead fading further away,
And decided he must be a creature made for night,
A moth, besotted, banging against the light.

2.   *The Attempt*

Surprised at a dawning white, white with dews
On spiders'-webs in sheets, on everything, everywhere,
A work of darkness whiter than white air,
There comes again the thought he cannot lose
(Like it or not) that world is continuous speech,
Never the same, spoken once only, always out of reach.

Curving above the mist the morning grows.
Webs dry. Their shrouding brilliance goes
And bushes have their inside-darks again.
Impatient and impelled he takes his pen,
Knows he is deaf, is a world, is talking to deaf men.

3.   *One Sentence, and Another*

'First, be clear in your mind what you want to say.'
Advice, in this rain and fog, which sounds even
More than it did at the time like bunkum:
For how can a man say anything clear when (say)
A gust of rain hitting a hillside can take him
So far to one side of himself that under a dripping tree
In an unpromising valley called Uncombe
He stands in his coat and out of it at the same time and clarity
Is not what he feels or needs and the reason
He knows is that he is alone and now not lonely;
As white columns of rain roll past him like sheeted
Spirits, others are near as real as rains are,
Whom he ought to admit to, though nothing is said
Or promised him in unpromising places and only
The eyes of water on branches are perfectly clear?

4. *Companions*

He talks to himself as he walks to an unfavoured spot
Which is boggy but windless, a hanging and desolate
Stillness he hooks on himself like a coat
    For this is his favourite
Place, and although overhung by kestrels he is not
Over-impressed by such taut-shouldered obsession,
Their hungers are smaller than his, for they look down.
    He is feeling his own
Possession there, his feet sucking out of mud
Under old thorn-trees (below these in winter each grass-blade
Stands apart from its neighbour, a separate green
    Isolation for sun
To shine at low season through each individual one).
It is ghosts he looks up for, as well as lit grass he delights in
And laughs to observe himself warmed by their non-replies.
    He is standing alone
Because he could point to nothing but drabness to see.
He feels himself simplified, soaked by their silences,
Held among lives keeping out of the god-kestrel's eye,
    His companions, the brown
Almost invisible presences, birds – that he notices
Stay at his side, on his level, certainly stay,
Though they silently shift to whichever side of the tree
    Is furthest away.

5. *A Clean Sensation*

Believing his dead invigorate the air
All round him, winging, bustling everywhere
(Not to be sure, always on his affairs),
One blossom-littered May on Bodley's stairs
He turned, at a loss, to address them: 'You known
And guardian affections – I have blown
My life. Lived it too much where you are,
Which is not my place. Nor this,' (the crowded square),
'Nor anywhere. Some help is needed here.'

Whether like nurses they came shafting down
Over the Radcliffe Camera is uncertain.
Hoping perhaps they would he crossed that town
Which loves success too much. (Though failure,
Undefined, he had not reckoned on.)
A clean sensation touched him, winging-in
Outside Halls' shop, pushed him towards the human:
He knew on his finger-ends he could settle for
One toe-bone from a certain skeleton.

Constitutional

Setting off, with John Cowper Powys's walking-stick
Towards Pen Hill (he attached magic
To walking-sticks, I to him) there passes the cattle-truck
Empty, which comes back, with a cheerful driver, full:
'Barren. They'll be prime beef Friday.'
Today is Monday morning. On the hill
I feel a need to name things, and know why,
To point my arms and stick and cry, 'the Malverns'
(A north-south scarecrow), 'those, the Marlborough Downs!'

Two boys' names carved on a tree are both barked-over.
(Survivors mooed at the cattle-truck. 'Always do!'
Those inside stayed silent.) On a village gravestone
A child's name we could easily read last year
Is gone, under lichen. 'Oh, get on
With your silage-breakfast, sad-eyed cattle, I shan't moo!'

AN ENCHANTMENT

(1991)

'An enchantment of the heart! The night had been enchanted. In a dream or vision he had known the ecstacy of seraphic life. Was it an instant of enchantment only or long hours and years and ages?'

James Joyce, *Portrait of the Artist as a Young Man*

A Ghost Replies

'Why – when you stand alone by morning waters,
Appalled that lives run from you, prudent hares
Put fields between you, bright bird-movement disappears –
Ask so much of me, for rescue?
My dear, my dear, here, as we know love
(A word for which we find we have no reason)
You have mine. But not my whole attention.
Yours I would have you give to a winter morning,
Observing birds that mind their own affairs.'

The Burning Bush

Has lichen, glowing emerald round its root
Which slowly grades to purple, to a skein
Thrown across thorns, a smoky purple hood;
Bramble leaves are leathery dead green,
Mottled, rimmed with blotches like old blood.
Four jet-planes practice looping, painted red.
Make pigeons crash through branches like plump stones.
Blindly sniffing with a puffy head
A limping rabbit matches bramble tones,
Mottled, rimmed with blotches of old blood.
It lurches, falls, bumps some yellow rocks,
Waits, too horrible for buzzard or for fox.
Beside the burning bush we wait together, cold –
Old blood, smoky purple, emerald.

Levels

If he could list all surfaces he sees
When looking outward – there a field of brown,
A yellow barn, and traffic moving slowly on the highway –
The list would make a mesh for what lies under,
A net that he could cast and then pull up,
Dazzled, by the light that has been caught.

He sees two curving boles that catch the light,
But also sees he sees what is not there –
Two ships so close there are two passengers
Can touch each other's fingertips and these
Part imperceptibly while water grows
Between their stretching hands, which covers them,
A blanket, till they wake. He shakes himself,
And almost sees wet spraying from his clothes.

For Saint Cecilia

O in apparently patternless
silences show
us clear the sounds we almost know,
surface of things your violin strings,
air your bow.

This milky mist eliciting
a violet and fawn
vibration from the silent-seeming lane.
Wet trees conducting swirls of white
till moisture hangs in beads of bright
like crystal notes,
while green on green
dark cattle-trails
are scored on dews
and elsewhere, helpless to refuse
as wings of dragonflies,

gaudy as stars of music halls
tall windowed blocks in London
draw the unseen sunset on
like sequinned coats.

Cecilia, who 'sang God in her heart'
(for each of us, perhaps, a singing-part?)
Cecilia, that ragged man
who stops mid-bridge below Big Ben,
is halted, rapt, as though you wrapped
a tune in him, his stubbled chin
so deep-sunk in his coat he seems to listen,
remind him now, remind us all,
remind us the unhearable
unsayable unsingable
silences are musical.

Surface of things your violin strings,
air your bow.

The Old Notebook

I warn you, Peter, should you look
at what I've scribbled in this book
    since we were last together
you'll be surprised among the words –
autumn nuts the squirrel hoards –
    at what you do not find there.

You'll read a song of winter snows
(or three, or four) as though the muse
    blizzard-bound, as we were,
had stayed till thaws, then fled, because
of all this Spring and Summer was
    you'll find there no reminder.

May think I carry in my head
so much constriction, meanness, dread,
  bleak pictures by the storefull,
that these can only coincide
with what is happening outside
  when the weather's awful.

For instance, yesterday a mist
draped shrubbery in white, like frost
  (new cobwebs, dewed, in layers).
I wrote of that, as though no wars,
diseases, prisons, others' cares
  affected me one jot.

You'll fear some stroke has left me dumb,
bucolic, inward-looking, glum;
  irrelevant, to boot.
It seems some others think this too;
each morning brings some short review,
  bored, of my selected

verses, calls them 'quiet', 'true',
a man who woos a rural muse
  and suitably dejected.
Not true (you know) but writing's rough
and truth is always quick enough
  to slide from under –

You must *believe* this! – as I wrote
'truth' the day was blotted out,
  came lightning flash, came thunder,
a sulphur darkness settled down.
When tried, the desk-lamp fuse had blown,
  the room-switch no use either.

So, great light snuffs a lesser one,
and I am forced to use again
  a language of wild weather!
Describe the bowl of dark we're in,
that is, a bowl turned upside down
  which now the south horizon

heaves, like a circus strongman
until a primrose rim, a thin
   cuticle of lemon
gap gilds autumn trees in dark,
leaves switch on like lamps, and bark
   is skins that glisten.

Peter, a seagull circles, slow,
is spotlit from below, its glow
   the livid sky offsets.
Mirrors as well as silhouettes,
each gives back what light it gets,
   and we are eyes, that listen.

Autumn

Why not a Sir Gawain alone on his steed in the Wirral,
He thinks, as some Quester inside him receives an armorial
Check-list of messages laid out before him by weather;
Why not a Sir Gawain alone with his steed in the Wirral?
For his flesh is the horse he is riding, or rather
His soul goes clanking beside it, where eyelevel
Pennants of trailings of spider-threads, gossamer,
Stream horizontal from fence-wires on unmoving air,
Catching afternoon light intermittently. Glad to be here.
Like everyone, long ago dropped into Mission Impossible,
Never defined, forgets what his Quest is and wonders
If ever he knew. So, for now, is observing the off-and-on
Morse-light from fence-threads he thinks he nearly deciphers,
Knows the full force of, but never quite reads his emotion.
Feels his flesh-weakness. Around him are blazons of autumn,
Bronze arbours, thread bannerets floating and, raucous above him,
Sun-gilded on azure, cold rooks indignantly circle
As though they were mobbing an owl, or for nothing at all.
Horseman and horse stand at gaze looking upward, the quarrel
Floats further away. He knows he is going somewhere and will die.
Now, into fresh silence comes singing – too yellow for Wirral,
An impossible pairing of brilliancies sing as they fly.

So sweetly they sing in their quarterings – 'Oriole?'
Frowningly doubting a sky of improbable chances,
Feeling a pang of belief. The type of aloneness,
Chivalric and flesh-frail, a soul in a vale of connections,
In and out of its flesh-steed, and baffled by imperfections,
Lonely of course. He talks, as he walks, to his horse.

Memorial Service

This rich man's autumn – trees like sofa pillows
Moss like furs on stones and sun-gilt crows –
My creepy gratitude is like a visitor's
Who has to go back to dingy accomodation,
His bag on the doorstep (cannot find his host), who goes
To be 'disconsolate in this Vale of Tears'.
But, if we're passing through it, our destination
Is said to be better than this one,
Which is hard to believe, looking on,
As though at another's fortune – which is ours.

Suppose I stay but choke back praises
(*Vere et dignum est*) at how an excitement in hedges
Can comb the western wind until it roars
Canticles? Coldly observe that in coppices
Some mossy trees have no moss around their bases,
Are maybe rabbit-brushed, or maybe air
At frozen ankle-level holds no spore –
Although so heavily cargoed round our ears –
No transcendental metaphors! Illuminations round a blank
Text, and no host anywhere to thank.

So, nature's loquacious logic made a game
To be reported back to men in cities
(Myself become the host) in form and rhyme?
'Art', and the 'Natural World'? The truth is
Neither matters much if only ours
And a few others', sighing, 'Beautiful!'

Then, 'I am a stranger with thee' at Larkin's Memorial
Service – the problem precisely – it makes my hair
Stand up. Never put better in three thousand years,
Says what I am: 'a sojourner, as all my fathers were.'

Chaos at Air Control

God without image (your masterstroke) our feeding, our
starvation, in whom I believe as I believe in air
stacked with potence queueing to come in,
cleanse our VDUs, our personal screens
foxed beyond reading with traffic of images.
Of (one night's viewing), families, frail-crafted,
rescue-hoping, clanked in pullulant gaols,
hair still spiky with hosed-on disinfectant,
(bunks five-tiered with capering welcomers,
Hogarth's Bedlam, bewilderment, 'Boat People').
Come in, and clean.
You can three-point land on any heart,
but ours your toughest test of airmanship,
our runways blocked with self-congratulation
that we still have hearts that feel at all,
at least for moments, till the next comes on
we cannot help or touch or taste or smell,
mere images. We reel, frail-crafted, over-burdened,
creatures only of eyes. Clean our screens
again to transparence receiving you, or we drown
in disconnections. Imageless, come down,
come in, and clean.

No More Songs

The only thing in the world, apart from God, that matters
Is money. Not the accumulation or the gaining but
The possession of it. Only then can we enjoy the world.
There remains the problem of those who have none,
Or not enough, who surround us (should we have some).
These it is difficult not to resent, and then there is God
On his only recorded appearance who was hot
Against having or thinking about it; also against resentment.
This is a puzzle: for when we study the blackbird
And muse on its life and our own, such leisure
Costs money, which it is dangerous to have and not
To have is measurably worse, so that envy
Of everywhere-blackbirds, heads cocked, watching us, turns
To a mixed sort of sorrow when innocent unmoneyed life
Ends in the jaws of the cat and no more songs for that one.

January Evening

It is the métier and, after all, self-chosen,
To waste a day and fail to find expression
For morning's special frisk, the way brass trees
Leaped from ribbed ground, and one-side frozen
Molehills were white breasted, like still plovers.
To know the soul's imperative to praise,
Not to placate a god who made these treasures,
Without a motive save necessity's,

And not one word, of fear, of jubilation
At a quick, kind unveiling, no good word spoken:
Of fear, because the page bears no true mark,
And light is lost – but never lost, the soul's
Necessity to praise – and hills of moles,
White breasted, still as plovers, roost in dark.

Blackbird in Fulham

A John the Baptist bird which comes before
The light, chooses an aerial
Toothed like a garden rake, puts a prong at each shoulder,
Opens its beak and becomes a thurifer
Blessing dark above dank holes between the houses,
Sleek patios or rag-and-weed-choked messes.

Too aboriginal to notice these,
Its concentration is on resonance
Which excavates in sleepers memories
Long overgrown or expensively paved-over,
Of innocence unmawkish, love robust.
Its sole belief, that light will come at last.

The point is proved and, casual, it flies elsewhere
To sing more distantly, as though its tune
Is left behind imprinted on the air,
Still legible, though this the second carbon.
And puzzled wakers lie and listen hard
To something moving in their minds' backyard.

They Lift their Heads

At the back of the hall of the head the permanent question:
Do the now-become-lovely, the unimpeded,
If they exist at all, still help us?
Avert if they can, with angelic palm, the car crash?
Prevent, with palm reversed, on the dangerous kerb?
Or even, like mothers chatting outside a playground,
Impossibly adult, more concerned with each other,
Are patting our heads with invisible unfelt palms
And, over our heads, call our skirt-cling, 'just a stage!'

When patient beasts lift up their heads from feeding,
We see in alerted eyes their identical question,
'Will he help me?' We recognise that expression
With greater fellow-feeling than we know
And try to pat their heads. They flinch away,
Are left to endure the grip of night alone
(For who in his senses goes to join the sheep?);
We see them in the morning, frost-caked,
Night-stunned, with no choice. They lift their heads.

Minimal Prayer Suggestion

Dread is easier to feel than God
Some days. Something about
Us rotting underground, or the thought
Of dust, ourselves, blown on relations' shoes.
Dread that there is nothing after all.
Many of us never thought there was.
Nor is there any good way to talk about this,
With those to whom it has happened impossible,

Perhaps. But most of us, content to roll
On rails when we have long run low on fuel
Of lust and first excitements, might at least be grateful
To the Great Anaesthetist; our dread
For most our waking days some way prevented.
That is, we guess, until. Perhaps until.

In 'The Anglesea' Afterwards

for R.N.L.

1

   I picture a yacht
each time I visit you,
   tethered and white,
abandoned by all but the crew.
   Which is not right,
I stare it out, instead
   again look at family
portraits by your bed
   you cannot see,
although you stare – your glance
   of a girl uncertain
her dreamboat will ask her to dance.
   We share a stare
in air, our mutual feeling
   grazing off different
segments of your ceiling,
   share your daughter.
You, patient, blind,
   wait for your call.
I stare to be kind.

2

   Outside, I breathe
fresh blossom in the street.
   Stand in a pub.
To exorcise that yacht
   I think how lapwings,
making air their own,
   fall and fold
their wings among the stone
   bones of a field,
and disappear, however
   hard we stare;
are gone, and yet are there.
   Your daughter's portraits –

all our starings fail –
   a three-years' sunhat,
and a wedding-veil,
   I drank with her
in here. I stare, and get
   no picture
of her infinite.

3

   Black and cold
that finite glass of stout.
   A streetwise blackbird
almost risked its weight,
   nearly weightless,
on my homeward shoe.
   I stopped, as though
a message might come through.
   An odd visitation –
the finite can astound –
   that unfelt touch.
Such touches may abound,
   sunhat and veil,
as your departure taught
   me long ago
and left me to translate
   how, black and cold,
death harboured a benign
   there are no pictures
for, and when a sign
   grows eloquent
it drops beyond my sight.
   Not comfort, no,
horizons further than that.

Natural History

These rain-slicked beech-boles know where they are,
As I do not; at least, not the way out.
I came to approve them, their top branches clattering,
Now I can see they are more at home here than I am;
Look down, as a crowd on the pavement looks
At a man with a grief which is no concern of theirs.
You have been standing here since the day you were born,
Through storm-nights, and in snow. Your still patience annoys me.
I came to admire, my feelings have changed,
And that should change you. (These I have passed
Three times, I can see my footprints in mud, pointing one way
Then the other, this is the third time, and still the trees
Pay attention only to wind in their talkative tops,
Their news of the world.) You have never been lost!
I am too old to be lost in a Gloucestershire wood!
Sweating, and – God – I've seen that barkless bole
Three times, no, four, I cannot remember – I have been
Following prints that I made when I found I was lost,
And not the prints I made when I entered the wood!
Somewhere, in some direction, there must be a road.
Or, indifferent cherubim, talking only to sky
Up there in your chattering branches, unable to notice
A swollen bundle you cover with leaves in the autumn,
You will stare, as now you stare, down at the peering woodman
Who prods with his toe, draws back, and then looks closer.

Invitation

Why don't you come in May,
see where the tide has left me?
In single beds when young
our lives not as they should be,
we know, but a drying wrackline –
this – we never imagine.
Someone has run my line

of wrack in fierce distress
(an unamusing fancy)
tossing aside long pieces
of coloured encumbering necklace –
briony berries, red,
some of them, as blood.
So, unsurprised I note
at the edge of an ugly wood
a flowered blouse, a skirt,
buried in tractor-ruts,
and further, sticking out,
a pair of female boots
(and note my morbid fancy).
We grow towards dismay.
Why don't you come today?

Afflatus

   The trouble with a wind,
    It keeps on coming.
At first, God's breath, a swelling,
Warm within the breastbone,
Outside and in, an air-grace,
God at play with creation –
   The trouble with a wind,
    It keeps on coming.
Atavistic terrors stir
Within the breastbone. Phoenician
Sailor, Beaker Man,
Knows when to run for home.
   The trouble with a wind,
    It keeps on coming.
A gust, a clap, a clatter.
Holes in the roof of shelter.
'God's breath', 'grace', metaphor
Dead within the breastbone.
   (The trouble with a wind
    It keeps on coming)

Wind-dazed, the Intergovernmental
Panel on Climate Change
Ponders Gospel warnings:
'I say unto all, Watch.'
   The trouble with a wind,
   It keeps on coming.
Sunset behind the Chairman
Turns a poisonous colour,
Those facing it fall silent,
He turns... 'Imagination?'
Black in a wreck of branches
A fluffed breastbone watches,
Whistles three syllables, then –
Chapters of thoughtful silence.
   The trouble with a wind,
   It keeps on coming.

Hope

For my thoughts are not your thoughts, neither
are your ways my ways, saith the Lord.

Solaces of fireside and book
Fade, as they become appropriate.
When he as a younger man withdrew,
From bafflement, to redefine his thought,
Beside his chair was time, a brimming cup,
Time, a kitten purring in his lap.
The worst of ageing is the loss of hope.

He marvels that his God should bid him strip,
Or now strips him; near-naked, either way,
Cup almost empty, comfortless his lap.
A careful, private man, he calls it clap-trap –
Old men think they've done with growing up
And loathe a canting phrase – when told to say
The *point* of ageing is the loss of hope,

Which is a blasphemy. Though he's a lighter man
When he obeys, whose griefs now taste of him,
Mumbled so often he's digested them.
Obedient, lets hope fall from his lap
Into a snow-smooth blank he's told he can
Without a footprint cross, not dint or coarsen
With himself, his hope, or loss of hope.

Cardinal Bird, West Virginia

Here where young men dulled, a blooming dogwood
Holds a bird too coloured, too blood-red
For such a Samuel Palmer blossoming tree.
Small cannons point the way they did the day
Boys here, of all sweet places, stood to die.
Inside a frame, a photograph by Brady
Of three boys twisted, one or two days dead,
Is stuck in the new-mown hay, just where they died!
Butternut jackets suddenly bright as the bird,
Faces slowly greening, not like hay.

Unwearied grass, unwearying creek waters;
And men are made of boredom,
Must undo, undo, our Shenandoahs,
Cannot see them till we call it down,
The blood-red bird, and only then we mourn
A blossom we are given, and re-given.

Calm in New York

Sometimes such calm arrives, but not today,
As polishes ancient pools in the upstate Berkshires
Till they could reflect a still tribesman wearing doeskin
Chewed to the softness of gloves, while singing
Crickets jump over his beaded shoes.
Sometimes such calm arrives, perhaps today
Will settle, the way the tentative ringdove,
Its head jerking this way and that, irresistibly drawn
To the drinking-place, glaring fierce watchfulness,
Humbled by need, is bent in the end towards water,
Beak buried, deep-drinking, its nape entrusted to sky.

Falklands, 1982

There are houses today that men have walked away from
They will never walk towards again.
Chink! goes a widowed chaffinch on the terrace,
Like a hammer on concrete it hurts a nerve in the brain
Damaged so often we quit the sun and the room.
It stands on a twig to see better, calls on and on,
Its twinned to-and-fro-ing cut short, is incredulous.
(Back with his kitbag, kids jumping up at the gate?
No. *Chink!*) With June half-achieved and eggs in place –
Chink! – is the sound itself of loss,
Not grief, but a clamour for all to go on as before,
Insistent faith, misplaced, and the cat
Asleep in blue shadow not even twitches an ear.

Whitsun

Here is a hawthorn explosion
rimming a secret crater, an auditorium
of self-applauding unseen hawthorn blossom!
(In fact, there was a bomb
dropped here, a German airman
voided one, returning home
from blitzing Bristol, where I lived then) –
'I', 'I', the quick return,
a flinch from the mysterious –
but we are eyes in a storm
of exploding exaggeration –
cordilleras, glaciers, cumulus
curds, with not a leaf or thorn
between a bloom, no room,
some turning palely pink at this excess.
A button-holing over-emphasis
of Whitsun blossom

shouts for our attention,
surely saying more than merely 'Season'?

Tongues of flame came down
above bone heads at Whitsun.
Strangers understood them.
Here stays Babel, stays
mutual shrugging non-comprehension,
gesture, pressure. This serious
communication of white flame,
affirmative largesse,
tomorrow will be brown
with disappointment, try again
some other way. I turn
back to the boiling fuss,
the white address,
in absence of translation
and use a human voice
to risk the best we can,
tentative, a '...Yes?...'

as when we sense a presence in a room
we thought was empty, and we ask, uncertain.

Resistance

In pearly sea brown seaweed swings,
Clings to the barnacled seawall, swung by the sea
Under the lemon cliffs. Silver and grey
Colour-washes, melting in each other.
No melancholy, long, withdrawing roar
Today. Sea licking slowly, quickly, shingle
Sounding tickled – which means pleased.
Light's language here a meld of grief and humour
Used by angels, maybe, saying grief
Holds humour in solution, like this water:

Saying – 'Heavenly-Hyphen!' What are the unwild
Waves suggesting, that I should suddenly say
What is absurd out loud, as though interpreting?
Or briefly understood, outside my head,
A bridge of punctuation angels use
To balance on, when, soft as feathers
Stroking our dismay, they tell their weird,
Without complacence, grief-including jokes,
And sigh, at our resistance. For in such vast
And welcoming dissolves our selves are lost.

Timesong

Brighter than nature, as though a Curator
Of Flints made a present, leaf-shaped, a white stone –
So knapped and so worked-on he pictured the man
Who bent over it, chipping – sun picked from the brown;
It is high now, the house-ghosts are melted to green.
If sun never moved we could never be gone.

211

Wanting a wonder he went for a wander
And caught the sun rising. It singled that stone
And drew the lost places, the angle it shone
At, on hillsides where once stood the houses of men,
Small settlements, traces, by shadows were shown.
If sun never moved we would never be gone.

Then it lit the far farm where they first were together –
She would know and not-know it, that house was its barn –
And from places so power-filled he should be gone
Now, as she is, whose music so entered his bone
He could go a dark journey to hear it again.
If sun never moved that could never be gone.

ITMA

'We'll follow the man with the big cigar!'
Unembarrassed they sing on the Victory tape of Itma,
Clarrie, Sid, Jack Train, little Jean Capra,
All the classless troupers of my childhood,
Concert-party soubrettes, tenors from ends of piers,
Brought together by Handley, the war, and my father.

Some of the jokes he wrote will do, but others strain
And break – 'I went home by Underground.
Fell down a manhole and caught the last drain' –
Its awfulness nearly pricking filial tears
Because of a lost, genial rhythm in there,
Unpretentious dactylics, a signalling thump at the end

Which the audience knew on its pulse. Maybe not good
Immortal work, not art, but I'll not hear,
However hard I try, the noise he heard,
Withdrawn, unjaunty man; the grateful sound
Those predictable rhythms provoked: frank gratitude,
An audience shrived, that stands and cheers, and cheers.

In the Middle of the Wood

Old footsteps I retrace.
I have seen your face.
What is sounding now
Soft persistent low
Near pigeon, distant cow?
Confusion is a pleasure
When the dream was you.
And if the dream untrue
Look where it brings me to,
This almost infinite place.
A different scale of measure,
Which leaves no itch to know
If what is sounding now
Soft persistent low
Near pigeon, distant cow.

The Belt

Christ didn't love those fishermen he chose,
He didn't know them. There was a job to be done.
Maybe John he loved – there's always one.
He knew their mixtures and he didn't mind,
Could feel disinterest because he loved
God, the Father, (you could therefore say
He loved himself. Like us, he had no choice.)
For the rest, he was surrounded by
Backbiters, plotters, pleaders
And ones gone soft in the head.
Like ours, his life was normal.
His kind of death included all of ours.
But what he proved, and said he proved,
And did prove – to see this lifts a burden –
Is that by loving no one
In particular, not parents, not companions
(Well, maybe John – there is always one),

He proved this larger love the loop
That implicates our heavy earth with heaven,
Without it there is none,
Proved this larger love the belt that drives the engine.

Written in the Margin

Hardware

More disturbing, every night, becomes the sky.
(They will not go now, words, in their proper order.)
Stars should be still, or stillish; keep their stations.
But now, when last green fades, and if clouds keep off,
Some move, creepily winking, then they vanish.
Orion and others have lower visitors.
Now it is possible, looking up at the sky,
To wish it would keep still,
And if it does, be grateful.
It was unclear before how constellations
Held our hooks and kept us steady
Before we went indoors, star-reassured.
Now cast up a hook and be dragged
Below the horizon.

Groundbait

'That's groundbait for the next lot',
he called the dusty drift
that lingered all week by the wall.
It might be
just enough to give the skies ideas.
So much passes over, looking down,
our lines trawl out in it,
ignored, and we look up, groundbait.

The Old Faith

i

Not in the frost-shadow of a leafless
Plum tree, nor in gnat-clouds golden with the sun.
Not in crocus bulbs set at the footstone
(Gingerly, lest we trowel too deep.)
Not in frost silhouettes, insect transparencies,
Nor under the patient surplices of green
Graves. Where then? In elusiveness,
Shared with all importances.
We do not understand the chair we sit on
Well enough to trust ourselves in sleep.

ii

'Elkstone Church – the secret glory
of these parts', said the stranger
by the Severn. I said nothing.
'But you *live* at Elkstone!' said my companion,
laughing. And later, 'You *are* hidden!'
Secret? Years after, a bumping inside it,
mops, wielded by friends in the village.
'Whose is the only grave constantly tended
with flowers, which has no headstone?'
John's wife said nothing. Her friend said,
'That's John's, isn't it? His mother's?'
'Oh', said John's wife. 'You meant that one?'
Silence, exile, cunning. What a provincial
James Joyce was. It's
the Old Faith.

Quieter than Clichy

(for Fred Perlès)

It was not because you met Rilke,
Or for Durrell's loquacious friendship, and Henry Miller's.
It was the way you tapped your temperate glass
Every time on the table, saying 'Yàssoo',
Which is Greek, in the singular, meaning, 'Cheers'.

215

It was even your small, perfectly polished shoes.
You turned the chess-board round mid-game for Bruno,
Lying unnoticed between you were eighty years.

We file out to the smell of gas-flues,
Thin transparent smoke. Do they burn us
Toes turned up inside our polished shoes?
A nervous joke, for you Fred, not heartless,
Who pretended there was no need to be nervous,
Who sought to soothe the world, by saying, 'Yàssas'.

Inishmaine

Sheep, heads bent, graze between flat rocks
like monkish students bending over books
invigilated by five swans' necks.

Severn *aisling*

Odysseus attentive to grey-eyed Athene,
Transfigured Beatrice lecturing Dante,
Who had muddied his glimpse of her granted him briefly,
As all must; a life in two worlds requires liturgy
Bridges, is balancing dangerously.
She and the river were singing this, gladly.

Walking up from your loss, your estuary
Sabrina, seeking your source, was a piece
of my life every summer with you as companion,
talkative, sometimes elusive, but only
at last when I stood at your birthplace and heard
how you sing at your source did I understand why

I had walked you, that you were an allegory
of what I believe in. Yours, like the voice
I remember, the voice in my long conversation
with somebody absent, and present as you are
Sabrina, sang that a sense of two worlds
is no treason to this one, is fact, as you can be

fact and be flat on a map and be mystery
when we are near you. Your sound was the key
to why you seemed female the length of your flowing
from calm disappearance to tentative birth,
for there as you gathered came clear to the surface
my subconscious reason for walking you that way,

upstream – to confirm the quick freshet I live by.
(A man on Plynlimon, queer as an angel's
the way he appeared out of nowhere and vanished
where not a rabbit could hide, saying sternly,
'I would begin at the *Source!*') Away
from a loss I had to make my journey,

your song said. 'You walk with a ghost and she,
like you, has a need to be solid, solid,'
(I grasped this) 'as moving water that's held
without losing motion only by margins,
as I am. Yours is the earth holds a ghost,
alive, and a river flowing away –'

such sweet intercession – 'You never will see
me again and, look, you are walking beside me!'
Flowing away. And towards. From your Bridge
to peninsular Framilode, Epney,
Ashleworth, Minsterworth – litany
recited in trenches by Ivor Gurney

which had drawn us towards you (a friend had come with me)
you pulled us both further, past cormorant mudflats
on one side (the other was gnarled mossy orchards)
through voices of Gloucestershire, Birmingham, Wales –
your own singing as changeful – till velvet
shadows of oaks in Montgomery

led to your desolate source, where memory
kicked like a womb. A blue dragonfly
dozed over your brackish beginnings,
your pool streaked with oil among cottongrass wind-bleached
the colour of sheep that huddled about you.
It hung like a fragment of different sky,

unexpected, a promise remembered, then quickly
as love (which seems like a promise remembered,
divinely inherent), augmented by oozes,
came singing in bleakness, the voice I remembered,
and blessing it brought me – exploding green margins
of mosses in colourless grasses, excitably

nodding fern-plumes you brush on your way,
as she did, a girl, through a cordon of glowing
admirers applauding, shy and excited –
oh, how could I not be reminded, not hear
what she and your river were singing, how world
is a language, and constant analogy?

Sabrina – a river-nymph turned into memory
of a reality – being divine
metamorphosis will not concern you, a blur
as fast as the balancing dragonfly's wings
of her into you and of fact into faith
and back will give you no difficulty

who endure in our world. For in moments your joy
is corseted under a road, put to school
in an acid plantation and only your voice
is heard, like the voice I remembered, rejoicing
in whichever world. Your escape among alders
and ashtrees, sculpting smooth rockpools, your play

is as youthful, but thoughtful (not matronly,
ever), as though a stern check to your gladness
had made you more able to bless by the way
stale wharves long abandoned and nuclear stations
of sinister silence. There men in white coats
furtively bend to examine a fly

for monstrous mutation, caught in their dimity
lampshades set on your birdsinging banks
on green poles like lampstands, absurdities. Barrage
could force you to service, past centuries did so,
their uses decay. Your mind is not on them,
your patience is deeper. And should the times say

that sexual love is illusion you equably
show it the hem of a garment to clutch at,
as unabashed, doubting but choiceless, for decades
I cling to the spar of an absence and presence
I heard in the song at the source and I swim
in what used to be called the Sabrinian Sea,

your end, no end, imperceptible entry
to widening silence. This on your way
you interpreted for me, saw no point in using
more than you needed, a dragonfly dozing
in marshes, then green intercession and song,
never ending. I turn, it is singing behind me.

The binding.

Odysseus attentive to grey-eyed Athene,
Transfigured Beatrice lecturing Dante,
Who had muddied his glimpse of her granted him briefly,
As all must; a life in two worlds requires liturgy
Bridges, is balancing dangerously.
She and the river were singing this, gladly.

(The *aisling* – pronounced *ashling* – is a traditional form in Irish, in which the poet is addressed by a supernatural being, usually female, who instructs him.)

Message

When you fell silent and still in a holy place,
Unwontedly so, abstracted, your thinking face
Averted from me as you stared at an ancient stone
Statue of some milky beast under Javanese sun
In Borobodur, I suddenly felt on my own,
Unwontedly. I, who tether my dreams, whom symbols appal,
Who as close as is possible cling to the actual,
Now wonder if such an abstraction so long ago
(As lives are counted) has led me to see as I do,
Suddenly, that the loss of my young self and you
Can no longer be distinguished; that when I yearn
For you, it is for me; in that sense on my own,
As I felt when I saw you were drawn by symbolic stone
Towards an impersonal form of entire concentration,
Which – for our link is unbroken – you want me to learn.

Index of First Lines

A box of sons on wheels   125
A hairy dog, house-size   146
A John the Baptist bird which comes before   201
A long farewell   125
A pale face, a hand relinquished at the schoolroom door   129
A square-skulled moonfaced monotone fowl   27
A vision invented me and she said this   29
Across the empty valley on a morning dark and mustardy   134
Ah! What creeping of late-summer shadows from the yew trees   43
All day a tidy wind has filled the air   17
All I want to do is sleep   127
An Arab on the bank of the Nile   155
An engine of infinite delicacy   128
Ancestor-hunting: an interest as sudden   164
As lark ascending   167
As often, behind the ribs, like a seal   168
As slowly they collapse   176
At Connolly's on Lexington, you pee on ice-cubes   142
At the back of the hall of the head the permanent question   201
At times it is good to be cold and ill and small   168
At three o'clock on the green   54

Baby, you fight the air, your feet splash it   110
Brighter than nature, as though a Curator   211
By poison maddened, the heron   126

Can you forgive the fastidious cannibal   13
Car, arrived in shed, disturbs the wren   97
Cast off in a boat without even a head for companion   43
Christ didn't love those fishermen he chose   213
Climbing a rabbity bank his breath smokes   128
Curled in your night-dress on the beach   12

Deaf and dumb lovers in a misty dawn   112
Despair as the beginning of belief? A doctrine out of fashion   86
Divers get me if they go too deep   34
Do this morning the dead, turned inwards towards brightness   154
Dogs barking. Men with guns   13
Dread is easier to feel than God   202
Dropped from the bubble-blown womb in a mess to begin with   33
Dropped fully grown, conceived by autogenesis   48

Edward, with thinning hair and hooded eyes   131
Elbows on knees, sitting to be noticed   144
Elizabeth Pritchard, Elizabeth Pritchard, Liz   174
Even has it in for skylarks   118
Experience we shared   89

Fair and frail, declined into a drinker   173
Feigns dead in winter, none lives better   160
Fleeing from colleagues to The Versailles   101

God, grant good manners and sobriety   180
God without image (your masterstroke) our feeding, our   199

Has lichen, glowing emerald round its root   193
Have pity on your upstart   161
He finds he wraps up warm to think of her   119
Here is a hawthorn explosion   210
Here where young men dulled, a blooming dogwood   208
How could we believe that   180
Hunched-up, muttering along the *quais*   47

I am oh, I am sick   70
I didn't love you, you didn't love me   50
I dreamt a love-story yesterday   17
I, Fortunatus, twang my string   149
I have done two years apprenticeship under   37
I lean back like a baby on this wind   122
I picked a cabbage rose   22
I picture a yacht   203
I think often of the time I was perfectly happy   57
'I think, you know   38
I warn you, Peter, should you look   195
I would if I could write new words for women   165
If he could list all surfaces he sees   194
If this is heaven I have the pain of a God that's in it   143
If you indeed look down on us from those high places   144
If you saw five birds on a wire and I saw three   152
Impatient with his task, dreading the sound   158
In a flat freezing landscape, the wind cutting their faces   133
In areas of madness softness is   141
In lands of perpetual summer   124
In pearly sea brown seaweed swings   211
In the december graveyard blossom moved   21
In the rubber dinghy on the lake   56
In this room where advertisements   31
In *Utopia* Thomas More   14
It is the métier and, after all, self-chosen   200
It's a pleasant night. So tonight I'll talk on the way   53
It's always the human   157
It's like a de Chirico drawing. The sun going   131
It's raining today, a dark rain   69

June her danaë shower lets fall   21
Just as the house For Sale you did not buy   154

Lambs bleat a lexicon of need   19
Leaves of summer   177
Lenin in Zurich given burnt porridge by his landlady   58
'Life has slowed to a crawl-pace. That's too fast   120
Living by water the welshman sang   34
Loss of a companion   179

Manhandled haybales not so yellow   175
Methods of dodging are as many   44
More disturbing, every night, becomes the sky   214
Morning looks out at the sodden air   166

Morning white as a sheet of paper   109
My father barely believed in the private life   75
My love is like a river as she flows   20
My own John Patrick, since you'd like to know   59

No legs. I must sit still   26
No one   64
Now thin grass on hills is tipped with rust   139

O in apparently patternless   194
Ocean-skin can cream and curdle   169
Odysseus attentive to grey-eyed Athene   216
Old footsteps I retrace   213
Opened and fastened, the empty satchel, so often   129

Patient bones in a sack   185
Peering for clues in dust on a brown moth's wing   186
Perched on a branch October   111
Picture a father running up a lane   130
Pink nightdresses in pink, night, boutique windows   71

Rain shall slake its dryness   33
Retreat upon retreat   91
Road-menders are flowers today, blooming in jeans   63

Setting off, with John Cowper Powys's walking-stick   189
Sheep go dark   182
Sir, these are very boring angels I talk to   121
Sky mother-of-pearl. Oyster-colour sun   49
Solaces of fireside and book   207
Some beaters in the mist go 'Purl...Whirrl...'   113
Sometimes my whole being   66
Sometimes such calm arrives, but not today   209
Stalled, in the middle of a rented room   158
Sure as a soldier to find the best place   161

The doctor in his surgery   65
The fire is out. The fire has to be relaid   99
The langourous isles, the tall bright-green bamboo   62
The lights beneath her skin are gold   20
The nape of my neck is crusted with sugar like a clinker   28
The only thing in the world, apart from God, that matters   200
The paper house was empty in the middle of the paddy   46
The rain is the same   24
The sea, like a band of elastic, snaps me back   35
The sky is blue and still   118
The telephone drills into a pool of silence   81
The Temperance Billiards Rooms in red and green and brown   56
The time has come for us to say we're sorry   36
The trouble with a wind   206
There are houses today that men have walked away from   209
There is a perfect   72
There was one who was perfect, who had   110
These rain-slicked beech-boles know where they are   205
These walls infect the air   30
They didn't like the colour of our skins   45

'This philosophy'   68
This rich man's autumn – trees like sofa pillows   198
This snow, thaw, frost, thaw and rain   153
Through screeching Mardi Gras figures, scorning a mask   39
Tonight a gale that scattered ships like grass   159
Turner, it is hopeless, Art! What have you done   146

We are two mice looking up at a cupboard of shoes   132
We climb above the green domes where we stay   163
We endow our gods with wrath but never exasperation   32
We move, tall as we like   79
We pray to a picture. A candle lit   164
'We'll follow the man with the big cigar!'   212
What do you see on the underside of leaves?   26
What is he looking for, crossing seas   83
When brightness leaves the trees they seem to fall   160
When day begins too lucid and his sun   23
When Goldie the golden eagle escaped from the Zoo   63
When they placed in position de Witter's 'Adam and Eve'   47
When we examine skies   182
When you fell silent and still in a holy place   220
Where pigeons waddle as though they've wet themselves   114
White grapnels pin our snowdrifts down   186
'Why are Academic poets   151
Why don't you come in May   205
Why not a Sir Gawain alone on his steed in the Wirral   197
'Why – when you stand alone by morning waters   193
Wind shrinks an iron rim on our ears   141
Wish me luck blackbird, in *appogiature* from roof-top   175
With a sore on the tip of my nose   25
Words are moles, they tunnel underground   178
Words in air heard   178

Yes, I can sell you a song if you want me to   37
You ask for more rungs in the ladder I   145
You come after school and ask me to write   139
You made me a tick in the rich fur of the world   167
Young people dazed with love in dying countries   16
Your words have gaps round, they work, John   148